Music for the Eye

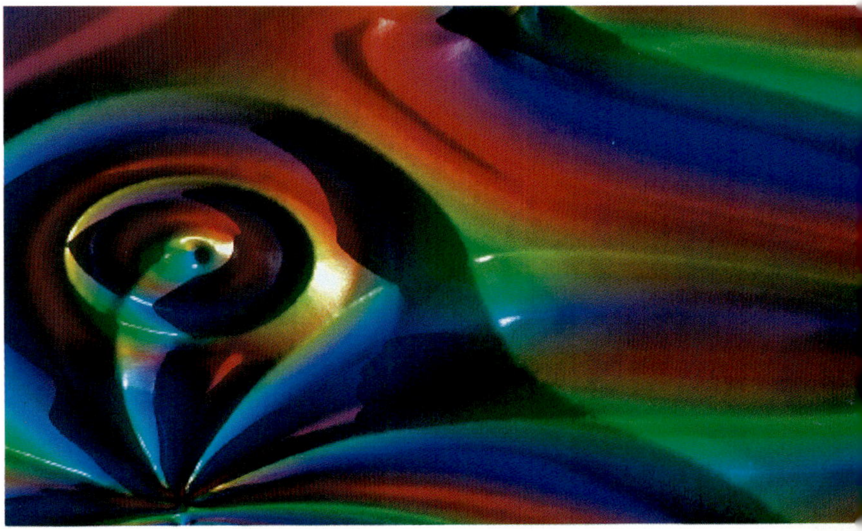

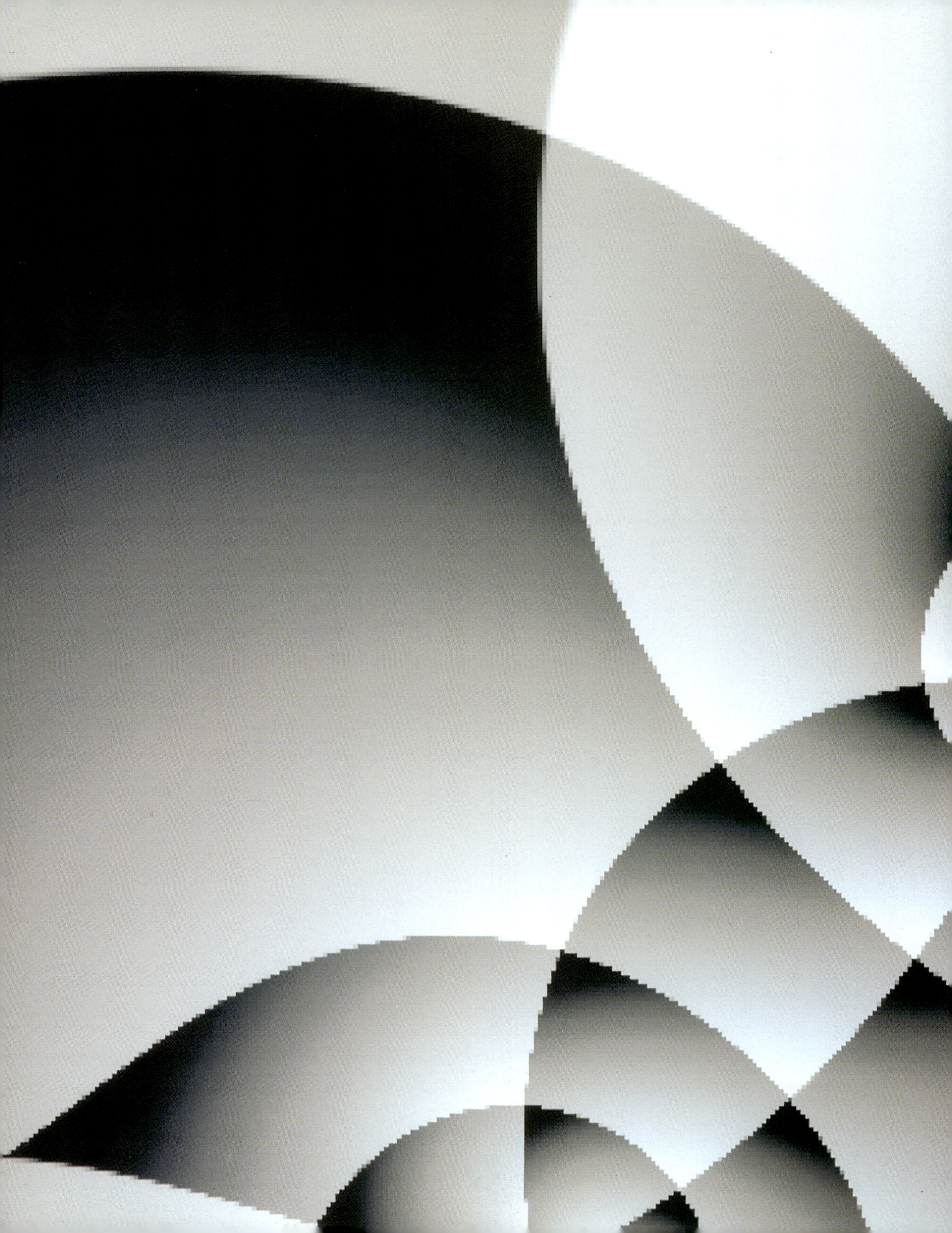

Music for the Eye

Digital Apparitions from Todd Rundgren and David Levine

CELESTIALARTS
Berkeley, California

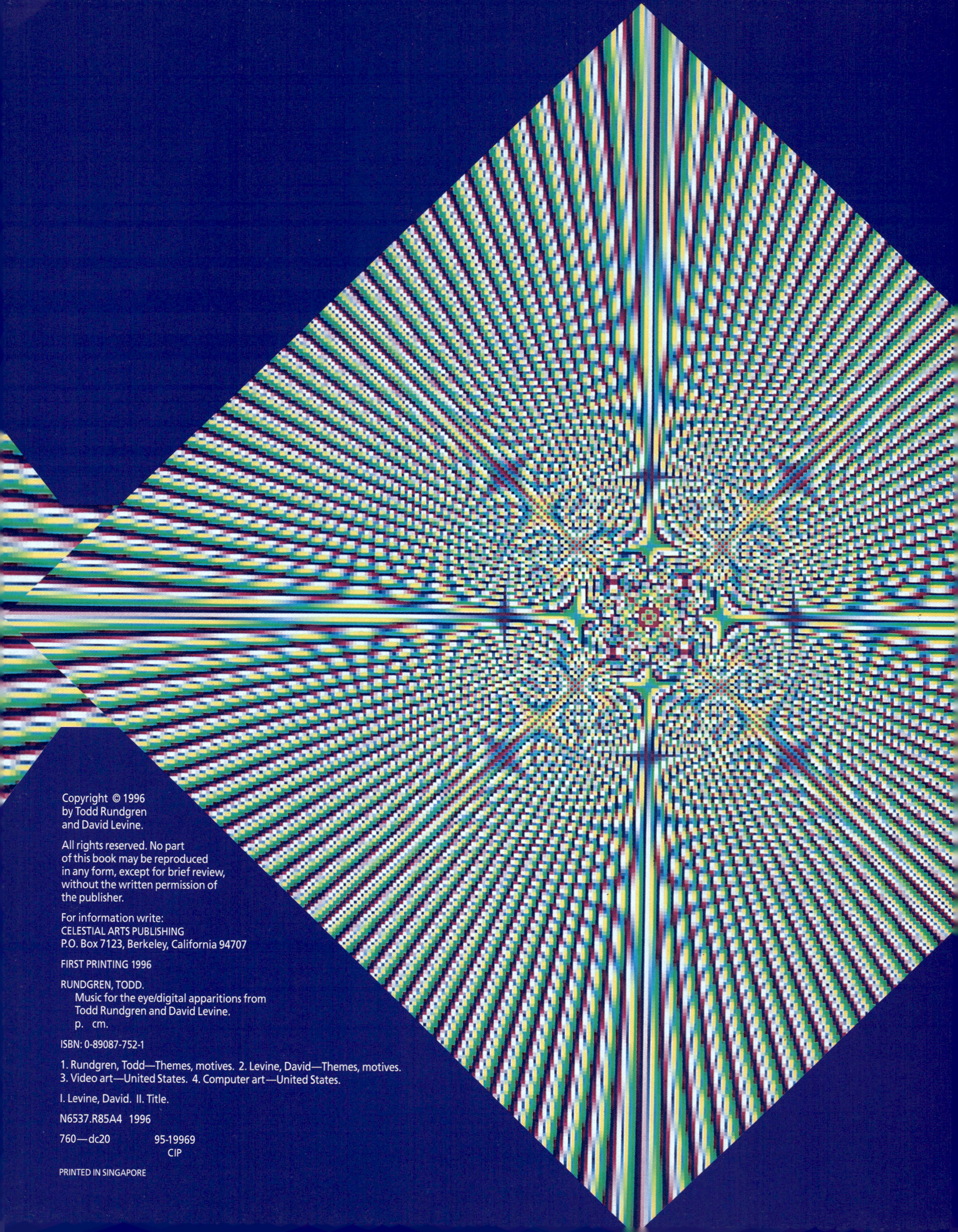

For information write:
CELESTIAL ARTS PUBLISHING
P.O. Box 7123, Berkeley, California 94707

FIRST PRINTING 1996

RUNDGREN, TODD.
Music for the eye/digital apparitions from
Todd Rundgren and David Levine.
p. cm.

ISBN: 0-89087-752-1

1. Rundgren, Todd—Themes, motives. 2. Levine, David—Themes, motives.
3. Video art—United States. 4. Computer art—United States.

I. Levine, David. II. Title.

N6537.R85A4 1996

760—dc20 95-19969
CIP

PRINTED IN SINGAPORE

In memory of Howard Jacobsen

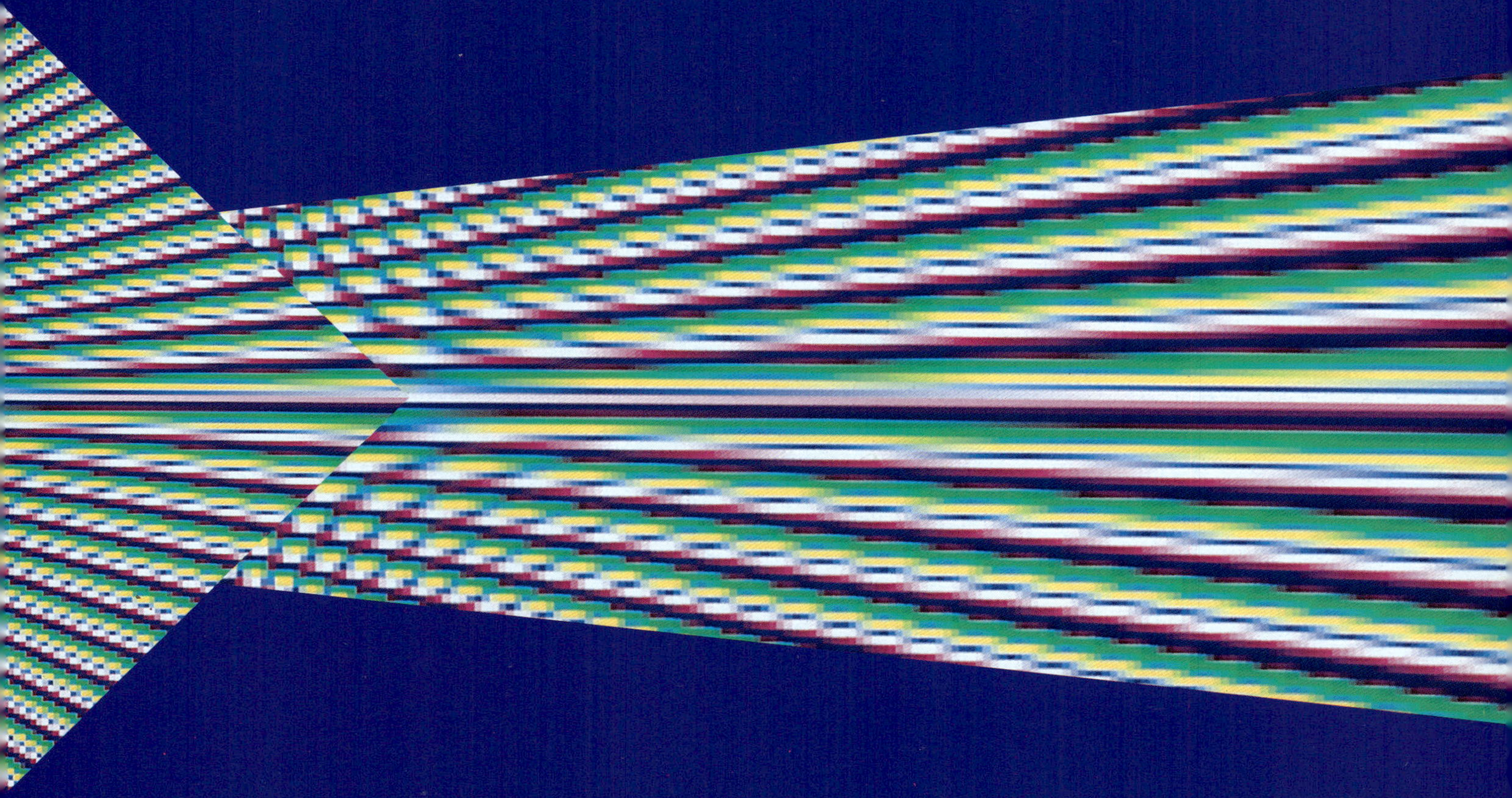

SYMBOLS FOR THE VERBALLY INCLINED

An Introduction by Nancy Kivette

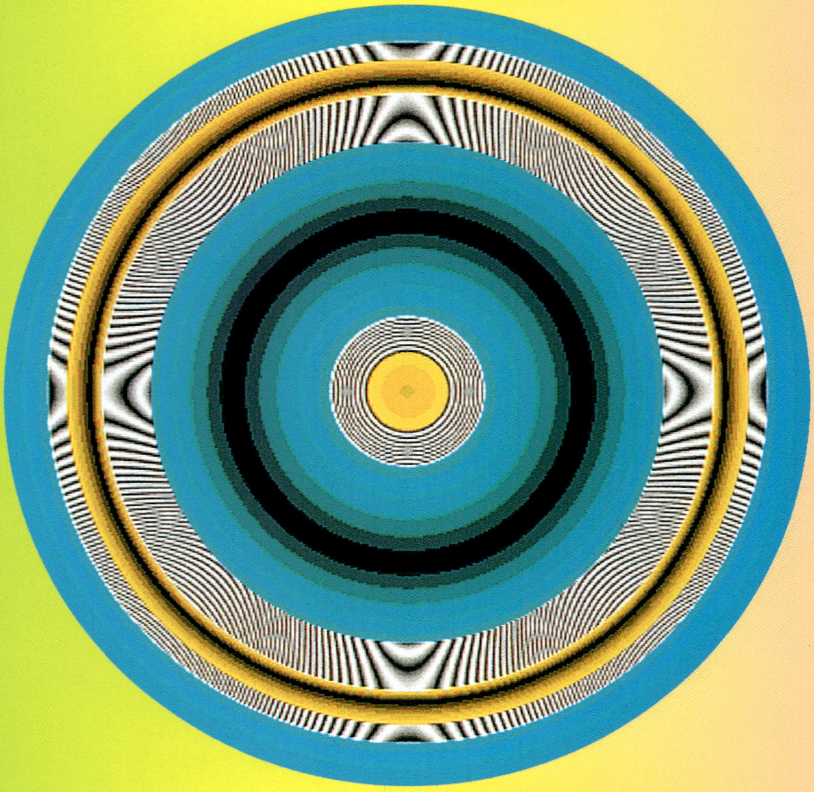

Music for the Eye is a gallery of graceful and curious computer art fusing the philosophy, science and vision of digital wizards, David Levine and Todd Rundgren. Together, they form Utopia Grokware. Their psycho-cosmic pictures splashed across these pages are quasi-randomly generated and not intentionally representative or figurative; they are instead meditative, and hopefully evocative.

"The whole idea of Grokware is to disrupt your normal flow of thought," says Todd, "essentially to disengage from your agenda." Utopia Grokware aims to "Jog Your Noggin."

For those who may be "disrupting" and "disengaging" for the first time, no need to fear. Most people new to Grokware art first marvel over its colorful radiance, "Wow" "Beautiful" "Totally awesome!" then inevitably whisper, "but what is it?"

Utopia Grokware takes its name from the term "grok," coined by author Robert Heinlein to mean intuitive nonverbal understanding. No text accompanies the art in *Music for the Eye* so that you may grok each image without distraction.

The style of art you see in this book originated from Todd and Dave's psychedelic screensaveresque software, *Flowfazer*, a taste of which appears in the page corners as a flip-book movie, and from *GrokGazer*, a video version of advanced *Flowfazer* techniques set to original music by Todd.

The organic and sensual character of the pictures is actually simulated by mathematical models whose evolution is described by changes in color and texture. "It's a phenomenon natural to the mathematical world of the computer," says Dave. It's also a phenomenon natural to the philosophy of Utopia Grokware. "Grokware in all its organically imitative forms, although based on mathematics, is driven by aesthetics," says Todd, "So it's not of interest to us what the mathematical purity is of any of the particular things that we generate. It's more trying to arrive at something that is evocative or just plain pretty or funny. All Grokware assumes that there's an evolving process."

An ever-evolving process himself, Todd Rundgren began his diverse career in the late '60s as founder of the power pop quartet, Nazz, and wasted little time moving on to a career of solo recordings and productions that includes such notables as Grand Funk Railroad, Patti Smith, Meat Loaf and XTC. In the course of some 25-plus years of music and multimedia he has been a presence in such seminal events as: the first live interactive-television concert (*Warner CUBE System*), the second music video to appear on MTV (*Time Heals*), the first tablet-based digital paintbox for personal computers (*Utopia Graphics Tablet System*), the first fully computer animated music video produced on a desktop system (*Change Myself*),

SYMBOLS FOR THE VERBALLY INCLINED

An Introduction by Nancy Kivette

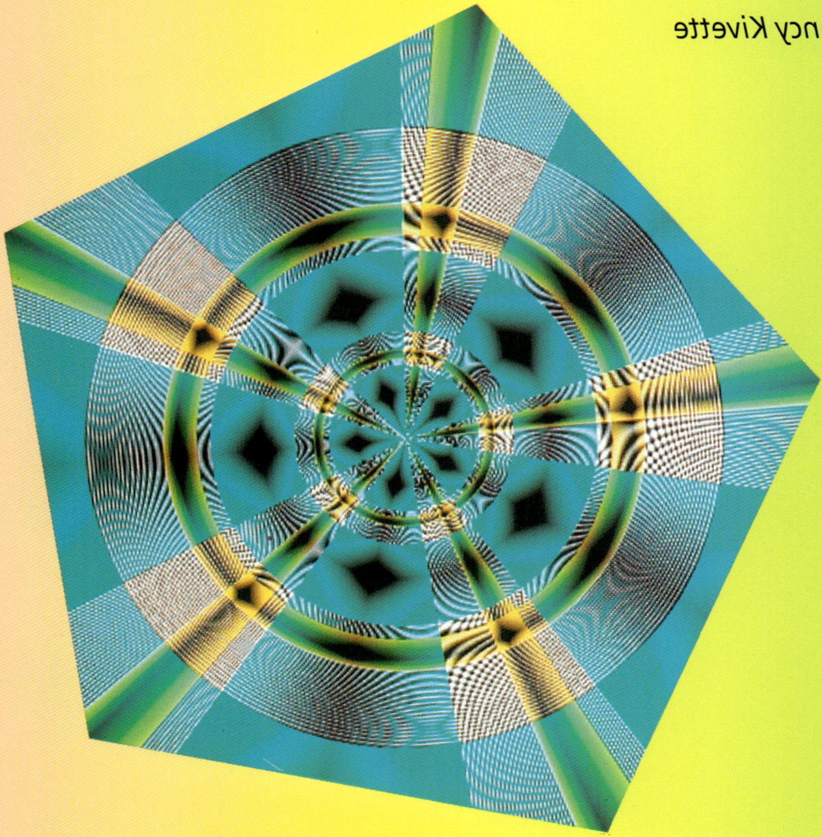

and the development and release of the first-ever interactive music CD-ROM (*No World Order*).

What thread ties these quantum firsts together? "When I create something, it isn't so much the large gestures that make a difference. They're so repetitious. In this world you run out of large ideas quickly," he says. "I characterize artistic work in little details and interesting juxtapositions. In that sense, Grokware is a simple idea, but it's these little details, starting at random, how we put the color palettes together, with a certain amount of chaos involved, from which the final piece evolves." It is this finely tuned yet organic approach to art that both Todd and Dave share.

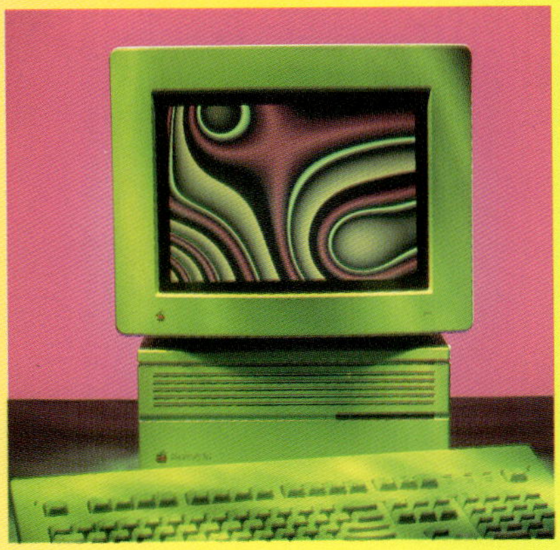

Dave started synthesizing computer art in 1977 with his own creation, the first high-resolution black-and-white graphics card for the home computers of that era, sponsored by the Itty Bitty Machine Co. of Chicago. He went on to study video synthesis with an early pioneer of the art, Dan Sandin of the University of Illinois. In 1982, after stints as a hardware designer and systems programmer, Dave drove cross-country to California in three days to become a founding member of the Lucasfilm Games Division. There he created the first high-speed virtual-reality computer game, *Ballblazer*, a cult classic with complex physics and two-player point-of-view realistic action still unmatched by today's games. Eventually, motivated by his original desire to create pure art, he left Lucasfilm to invent the computer visuals he had mused over for years.

Grokware began with trains, puddles and silk moiré. In his early 20s, Dave began seeing things. He noticed a certain pattern in wood grain and on the surfaces of oily puddles and silk fabric. From the train on the way to school in Chicago, he passed by buildings where he saw window screens interfering with their own reflections, producing a mesmerizing motion in black and white. In order to translate the transcendent quality of this motion on the windows to an 8-bit color Macintosh II, Dave "based the program's geometry on an essential physical principle, electromagnetic fields, the basis of all phenomena between nuclear and cosmic," he says. The effect was stunning — Earth's first computer-generated, random, real-time video synthesis, full-screen, color-cycling lava lamp/light show: *Flowfazer.*

Unfortunately it was 1988 and "At the time it was created, there was no other animation product for the Macintosh or

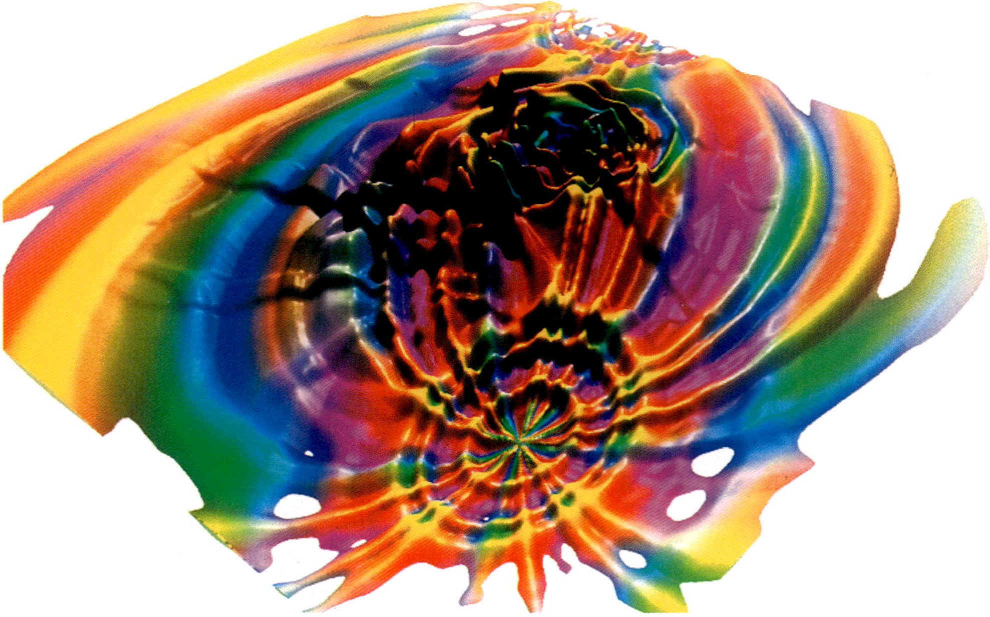

similar machines that was meant specifically for entertainment and meditation with no utilitarian purpose," says Dave.

Coincidentally, Todd was evangelizing his own program, a document-based graphical operating environment called *Hypercode*. Like the primordial stage of *Flowfazer,* publishers were afraid to touch it, because they just didn't grok it.

Flowfazer may never have come to market without the facilitation of Michele Gray, witness to the eponymous first encounter of Todd and Dave at an informal gathering of computer graphics nuts: Dave says Todd was "ornery," Todd says Dave was "a wise guy," and Michele says they were both "brilliant and creative…curmudgeons." Todd and Dave soon discovered a common computer vision: synthesizing "videodrugs." "Something that gets to the inside of your brain because of the perfection of the mathematics," according to Dave, something with an "implicitly kinetic quality about it, generated from a process," according to Todd, while Michele recognized the beginning of an alternative software company. In the fall of 1989, Utopia Grokware opened its peculiar doors in Sausalito, California.

Dave and Todd's first collaborative effort was the free program *Eyelixir* that blasts the screen with TV-type snow. An example of videodrugs for the Mac, it induced visual hallucinations in the viewer — precisely what the digital dazzle doctors prescribed. *Eyelixir* also advertised Utopia Grokware's statement of purpose:

Are You a Victim of Shrinking Digital Diversity?
Do You Miss That Stimulating Buzz You Used to
Expect From Your Man-Machine Interactions?
Lost That Lovin' Feeling?
Let Utopia Grokware Jog Your Noggin.
We Will Provide You With the Tools to Rebuild
Your Mental Manifesto.
Eyelixir Is a Free Sample.
You'll Want More.

With *Eyelixir* set free on its subversive mission to initiate the masses, Todd worked with Dave to further develop *Flowfazer* into a real product. In 1990 the Grokware Gurus released *Flowfazer*, asserting on the package, "Some things defy description" and "It should be legal to alter your mind." To reach a computerless audience, Todd and Dave switched to videotape and recorded *GrokGazer* that same year. Perhaps you'll recognize *GrokGazer's* influence in some more recent TV identification or promo spots.

Furthering its seduction of the mass market, Utopia Grokware then spun off a kaleidoscope of print media. The first image appeared in 1991 as a poster titled, "Scope." Its surprising success introduced the experience to an even wider

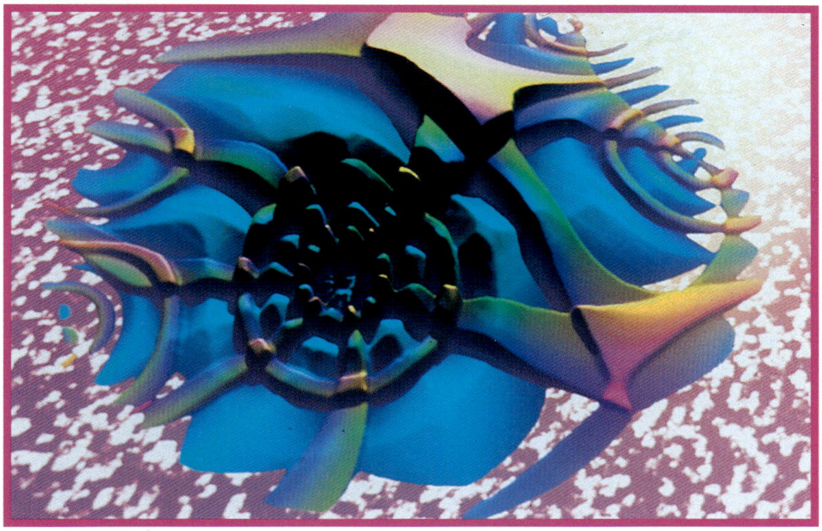

audience, and for the first time, captured forever a meditative moment from the intrinsically elusive expression of kinetic Grokware. Two versions of the second poster, "Zone," were printed, one with felt flocking over the black ink (like velvet Elvis paintings). The third poster, "Prism," optically twists and pulsates. This initial trickle of Grokware turned into a torrent of posters, calendars, jigsaw puzzles and book covers, culminating thus far in *Music for the Eye*.

According to Dave, the popularity of the printed images is partly due to their implied kinetic quality. "Even the static images produce a sensation of movement," he says, "they don't sit still on a page." Todd adds, "I think Grokware also elicits a primal response. It looks like something that people naturally respond to, like the lava lamp. As goofy as the lava lamp was, that amorphous blobbing gets down to cell memory."

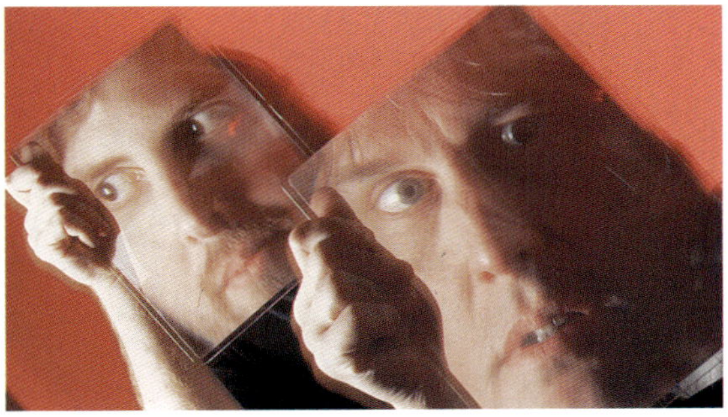

DAVID TODD

The images in *Music for the Eye* have been compared to psychedelic expressions of the '60s: liquid light shows, op art, and tie-dye effects. Most of the unique designs, refined definition and coloration you see on these pages were produced by Michele who uses proprietary tools custom made for her by Todd and Dave to "cast" an image (randomly determine its shape), and "color" it (choose and apply a palette of colors). Because *Flowfazer* images are infinitely variable and non-recurring, her task is to recognize and capture that one fantastic accident when it materializes. Michele's latest experiment involved a "mathamatical error" that turned out a beautiful form she calls, "New Bud." Todd enhanced some of the images with 3-D tools to amplify depth, and Dave conjured up some anthropomorphic images he calls "Alien Buddha," "Flo Picasso," and "The Demon" which appears on the flip-book movie.

Like any good abstract art, these pictures can be continually transportive. "In a world that's trying to force an agenda on you, Grokware can put you in a different place," says Todd, "A place where the blissfulness and detachment of the imagery is like dipping your brain in cool water." So disengage. Turn the page, and chill.

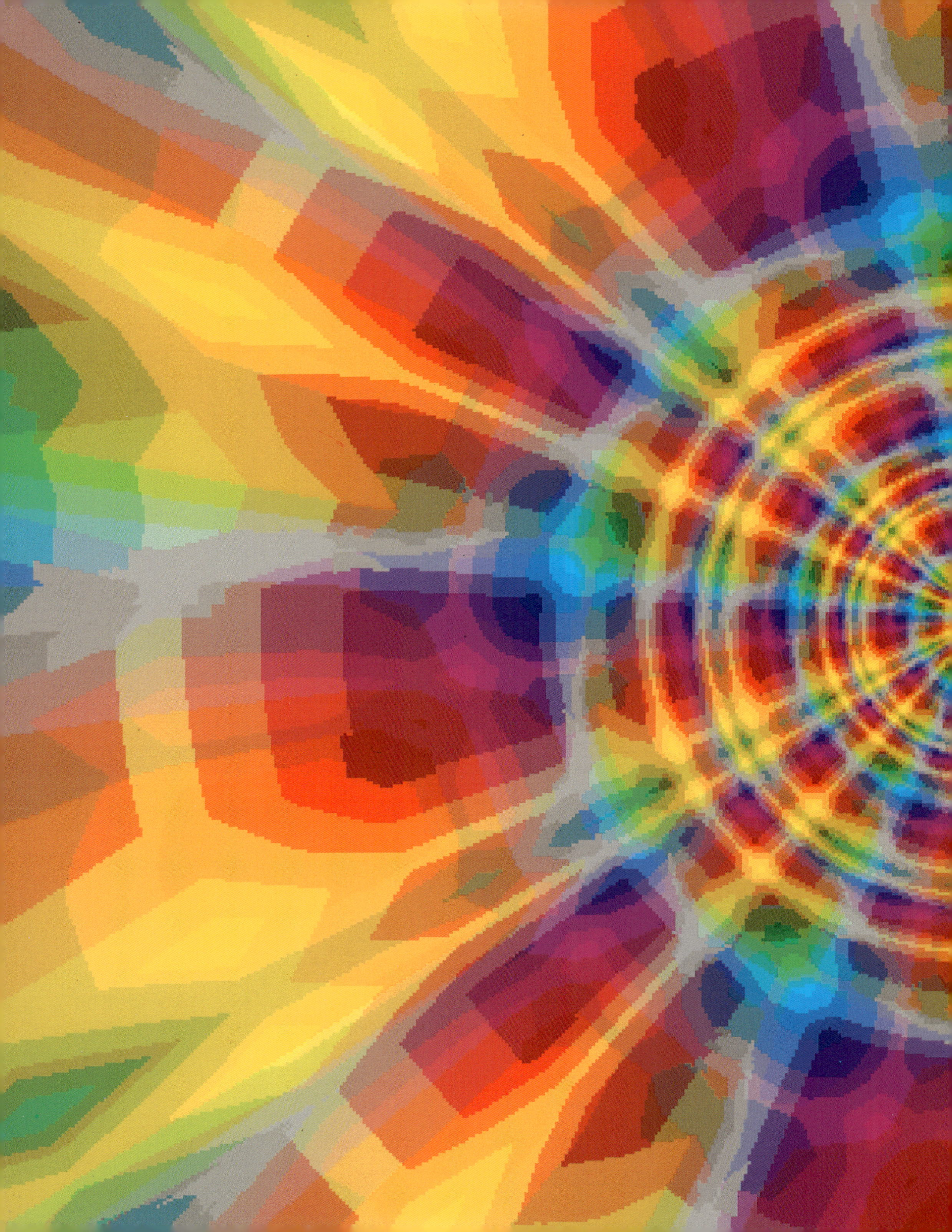

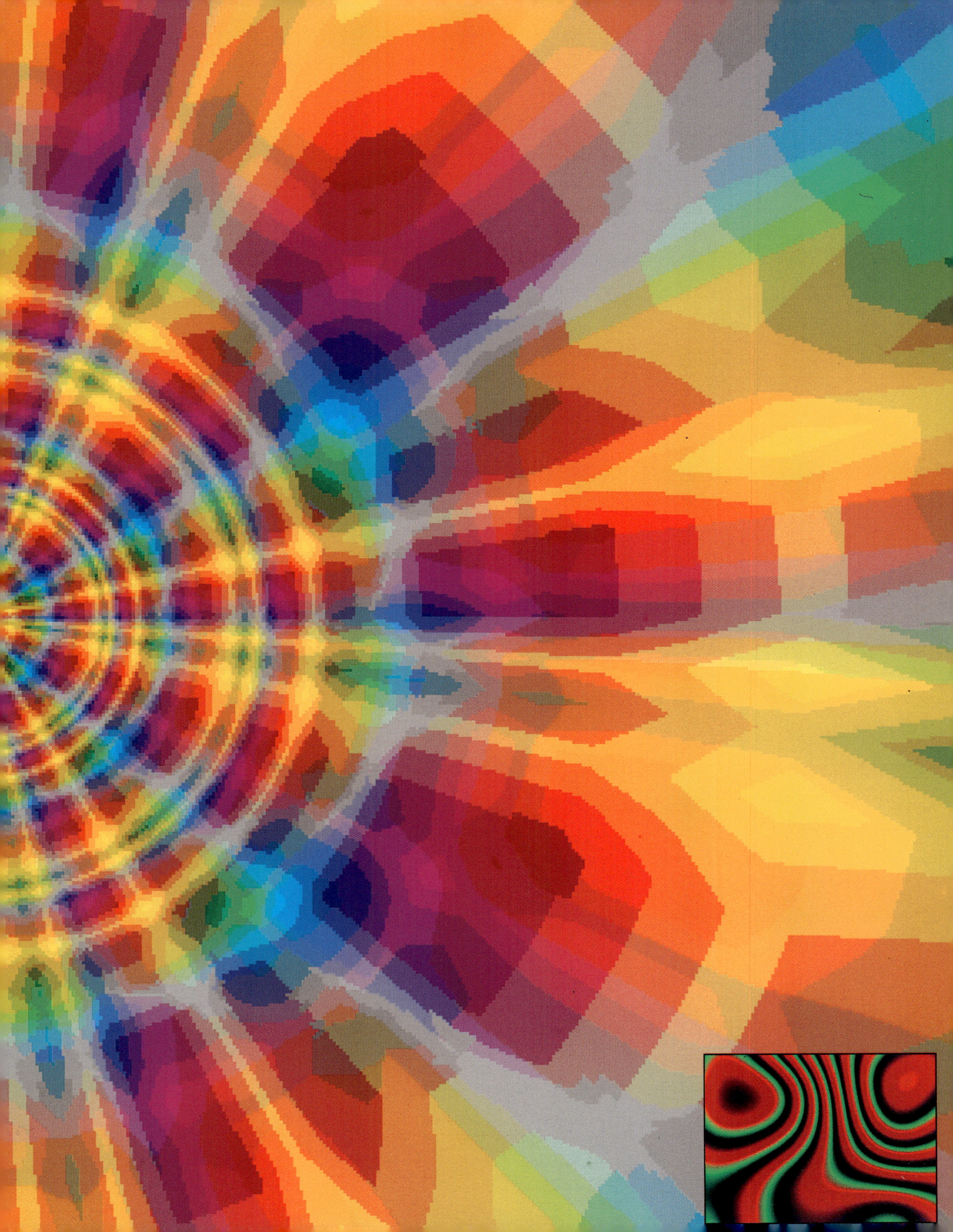

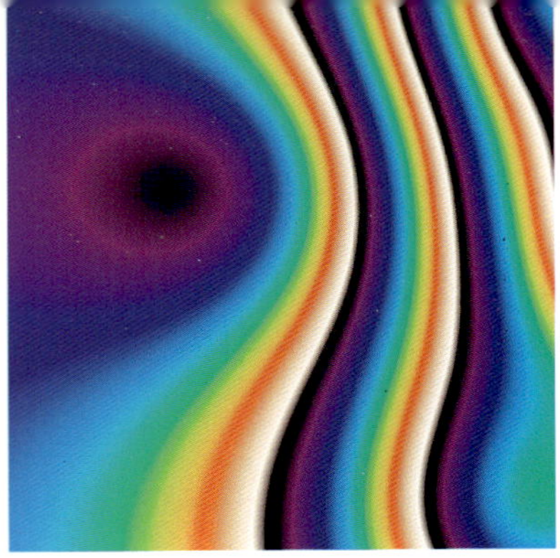

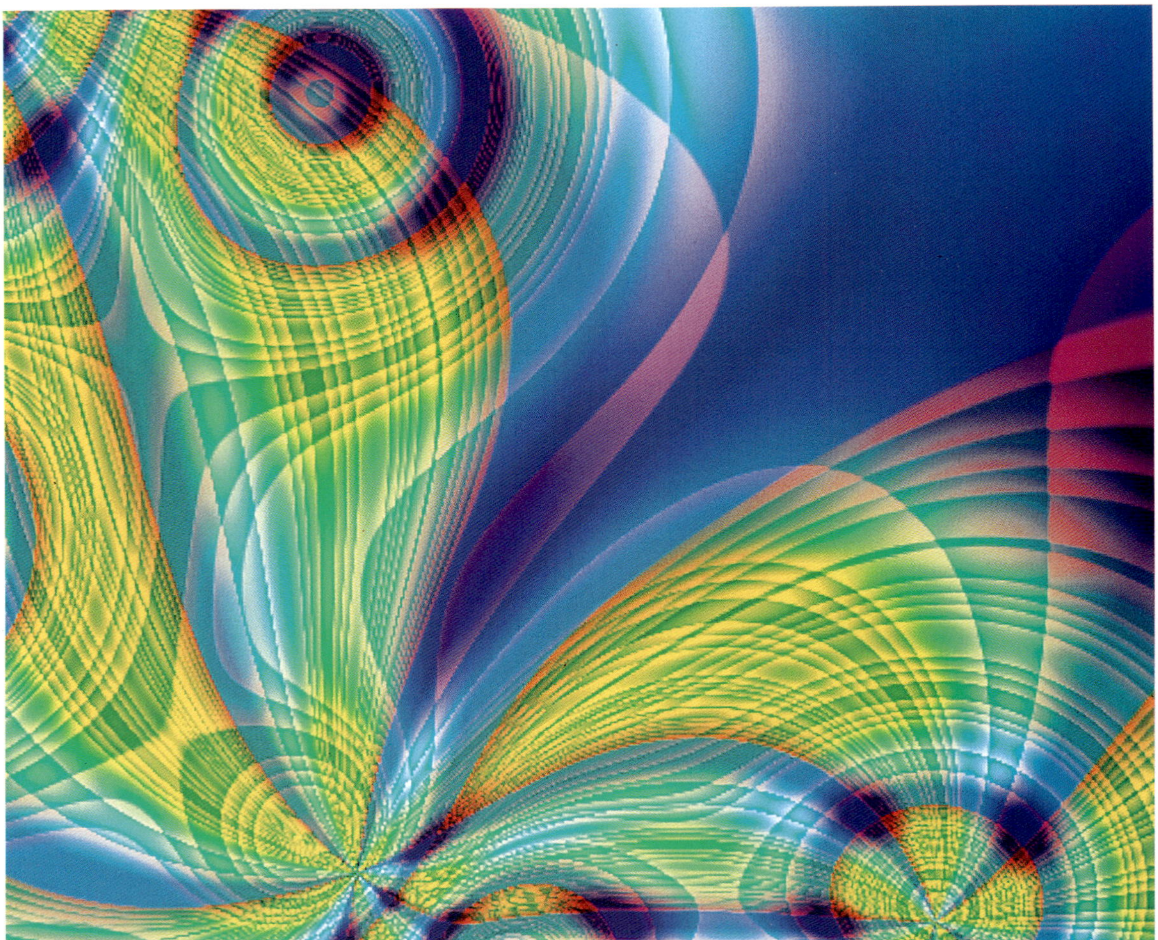

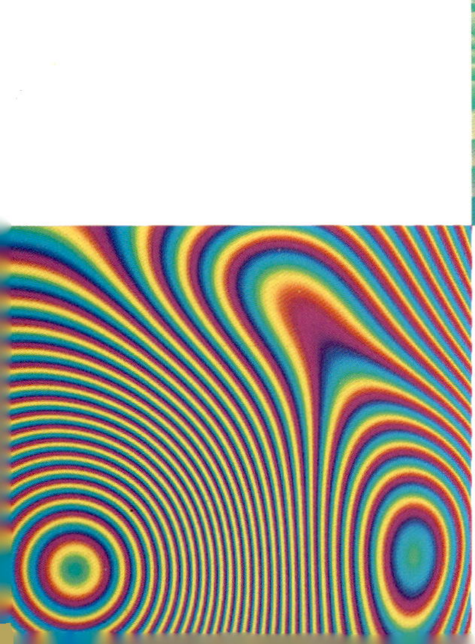

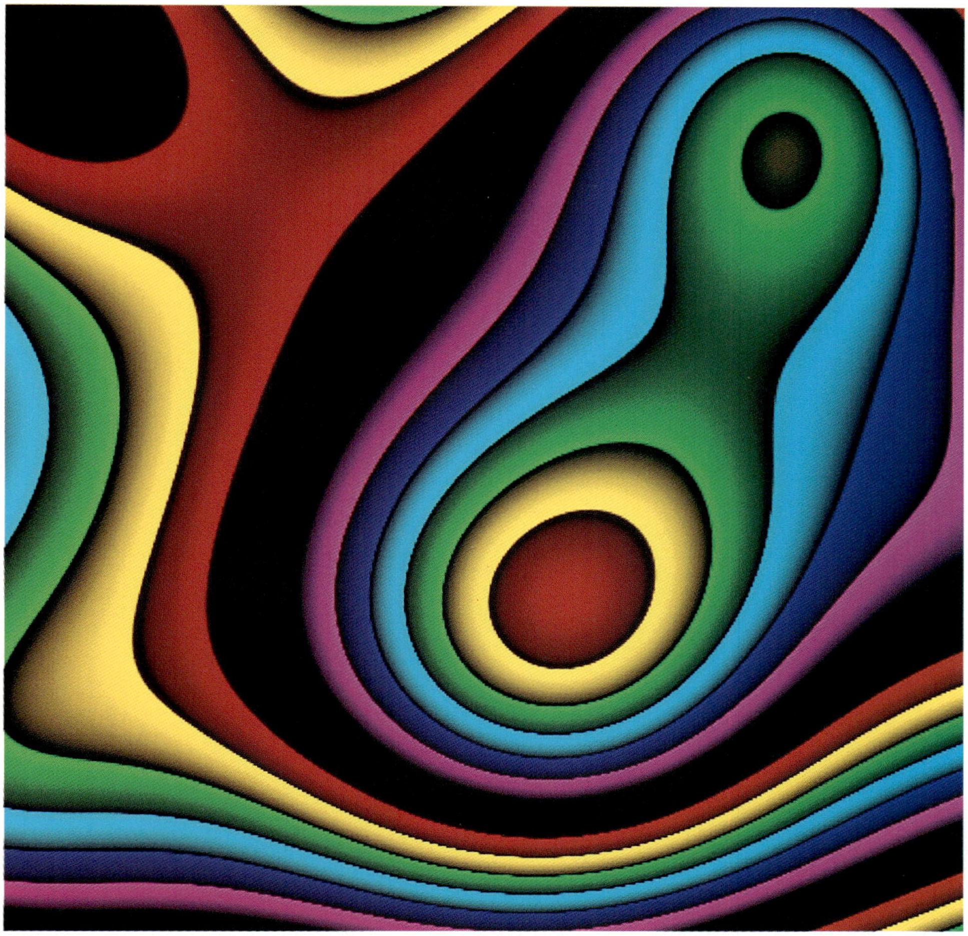

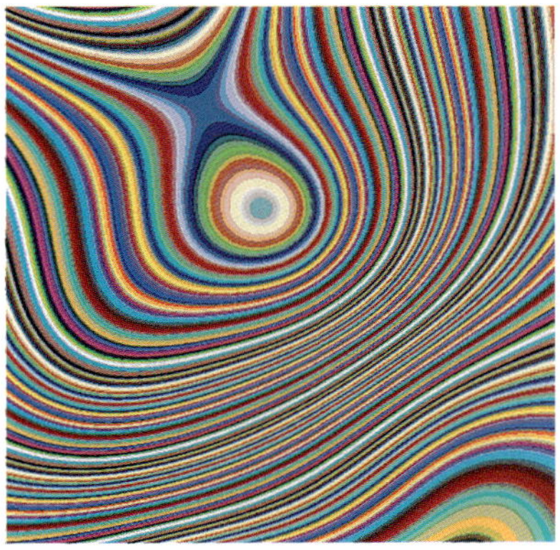

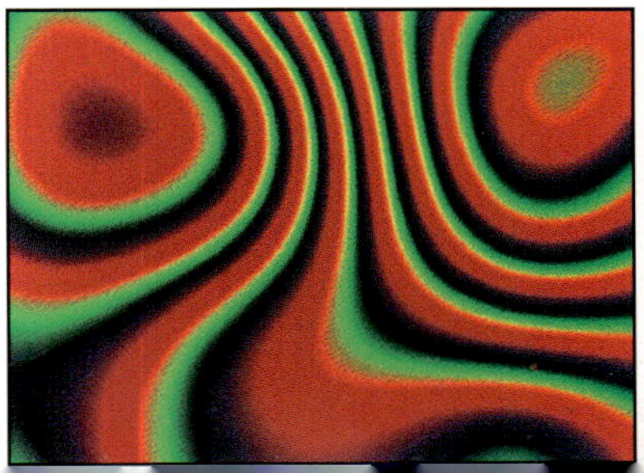

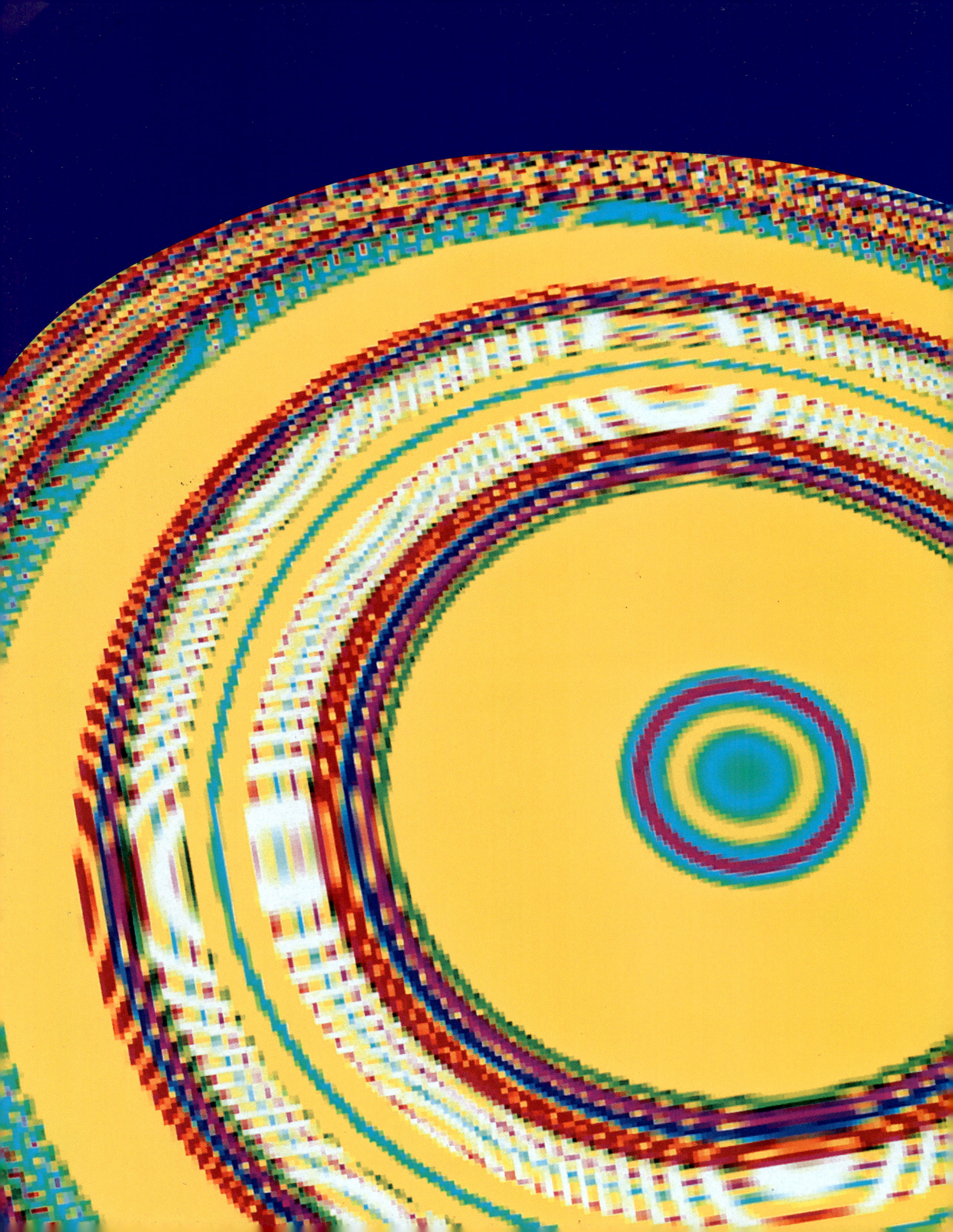

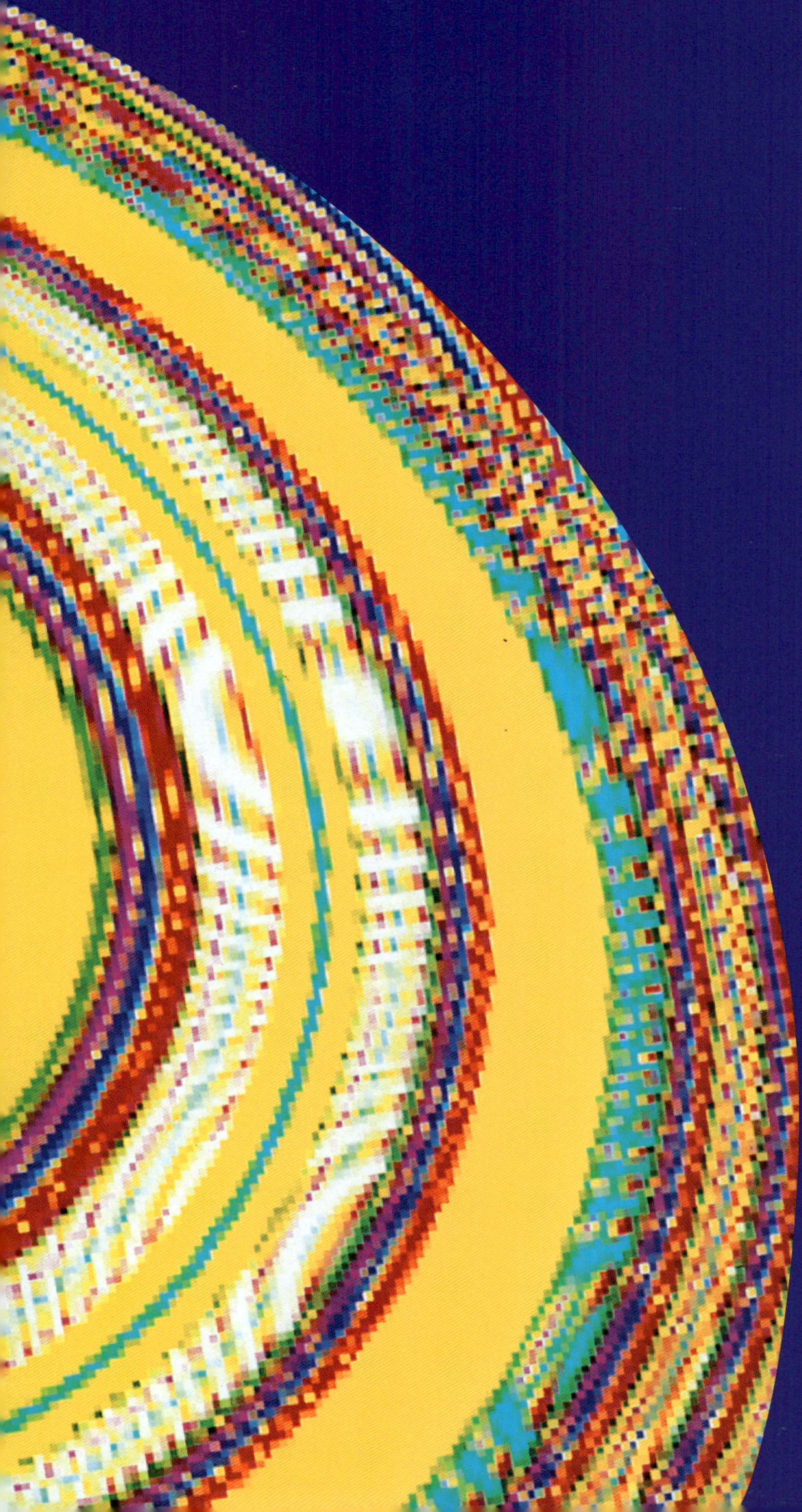
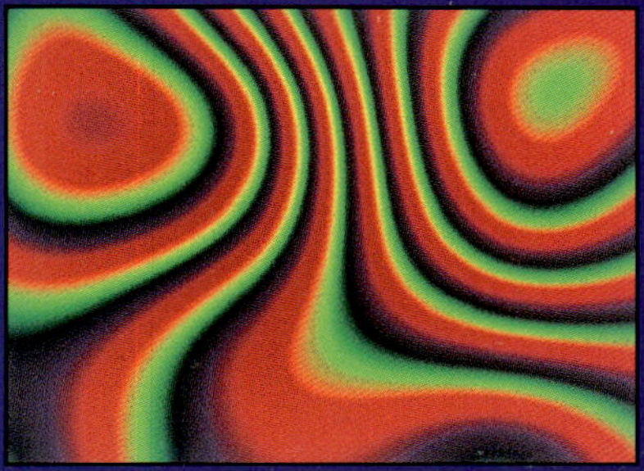

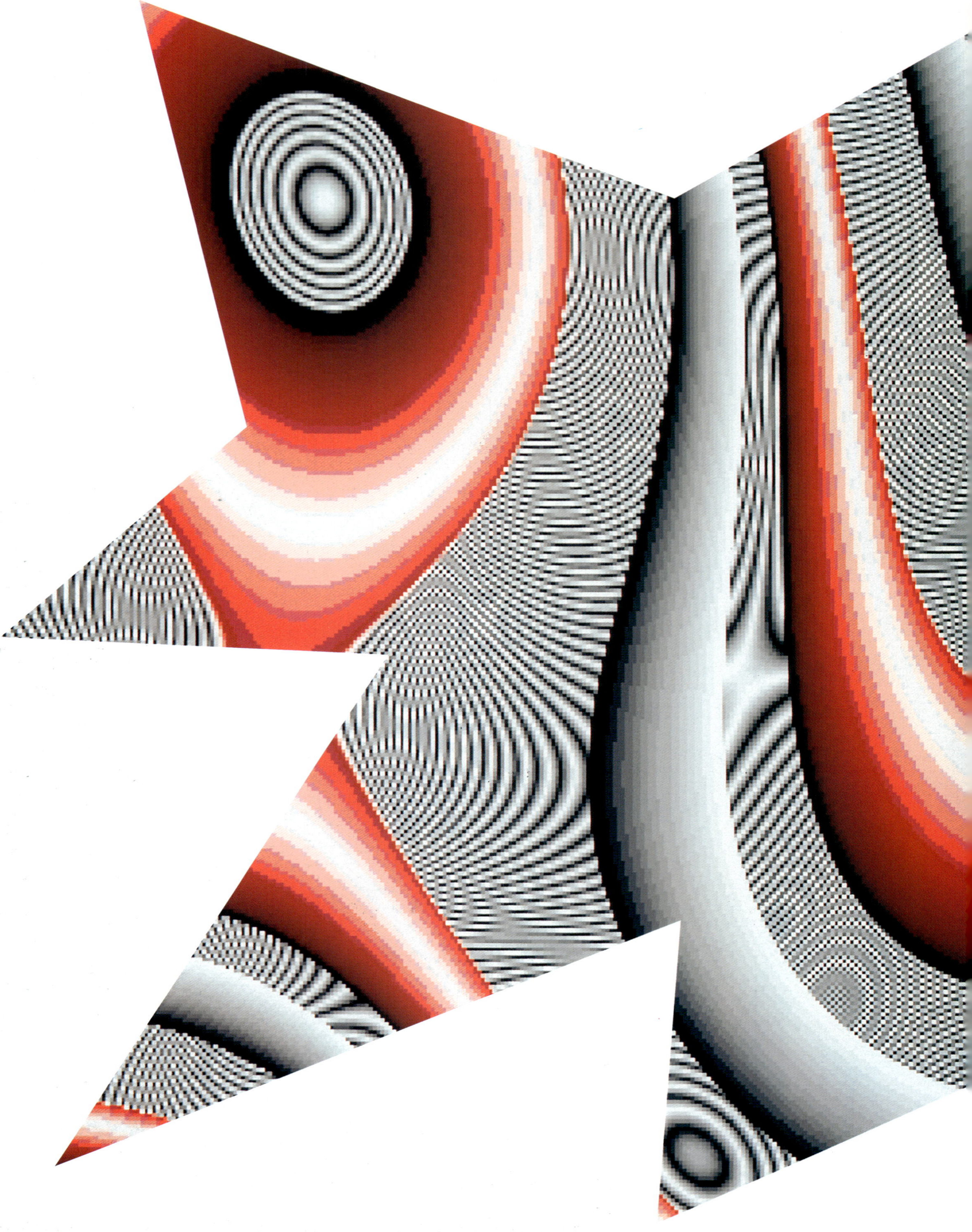

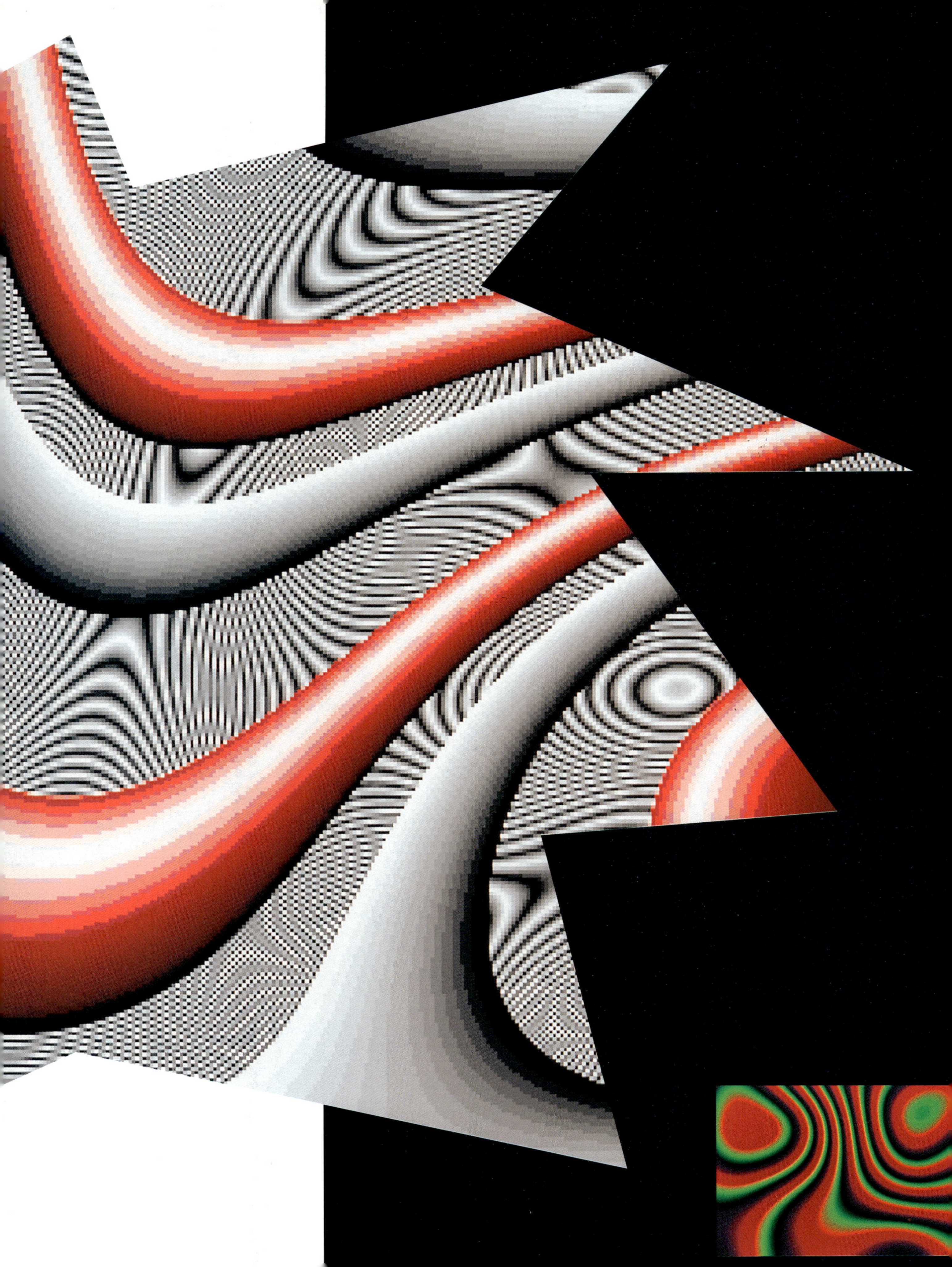

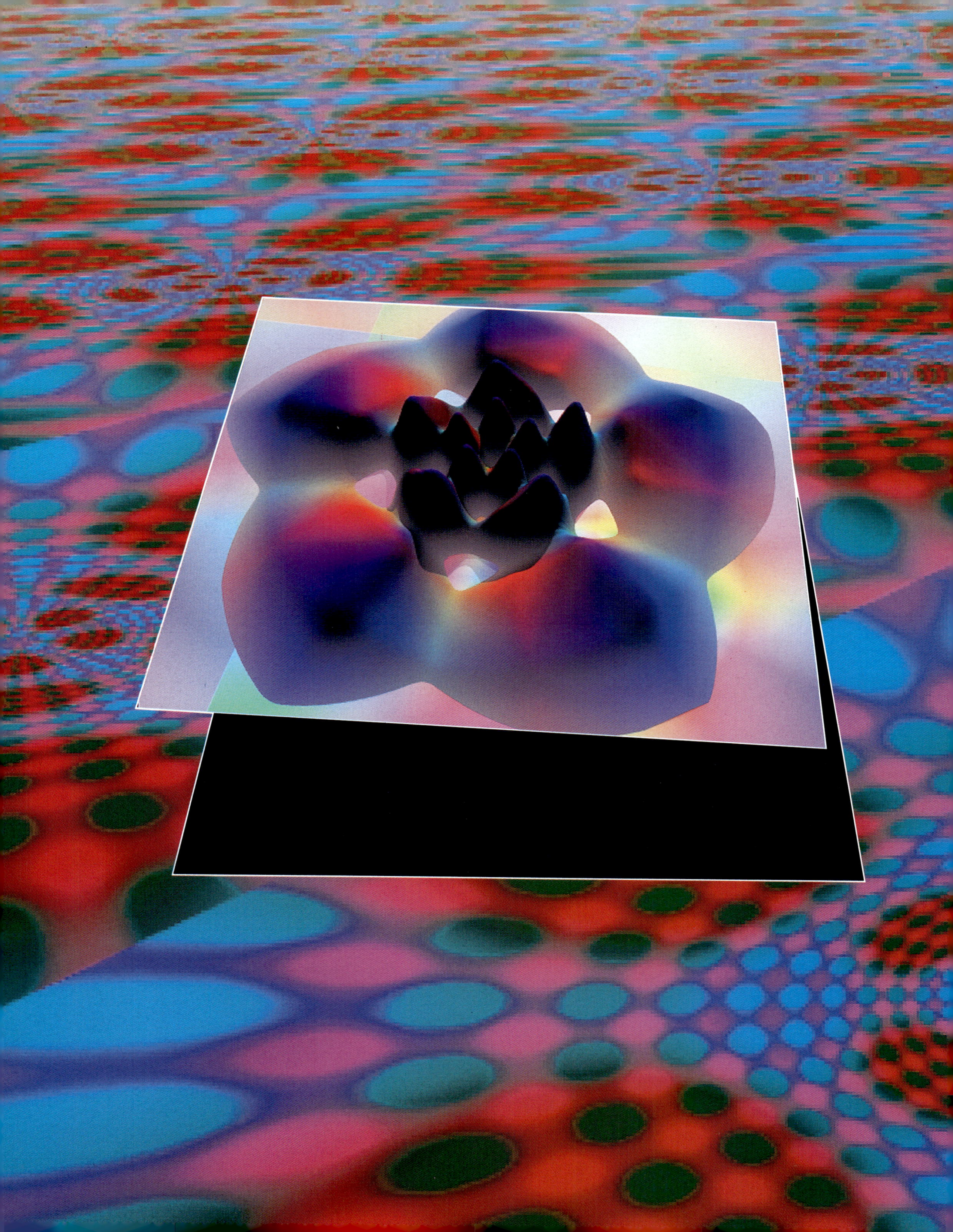

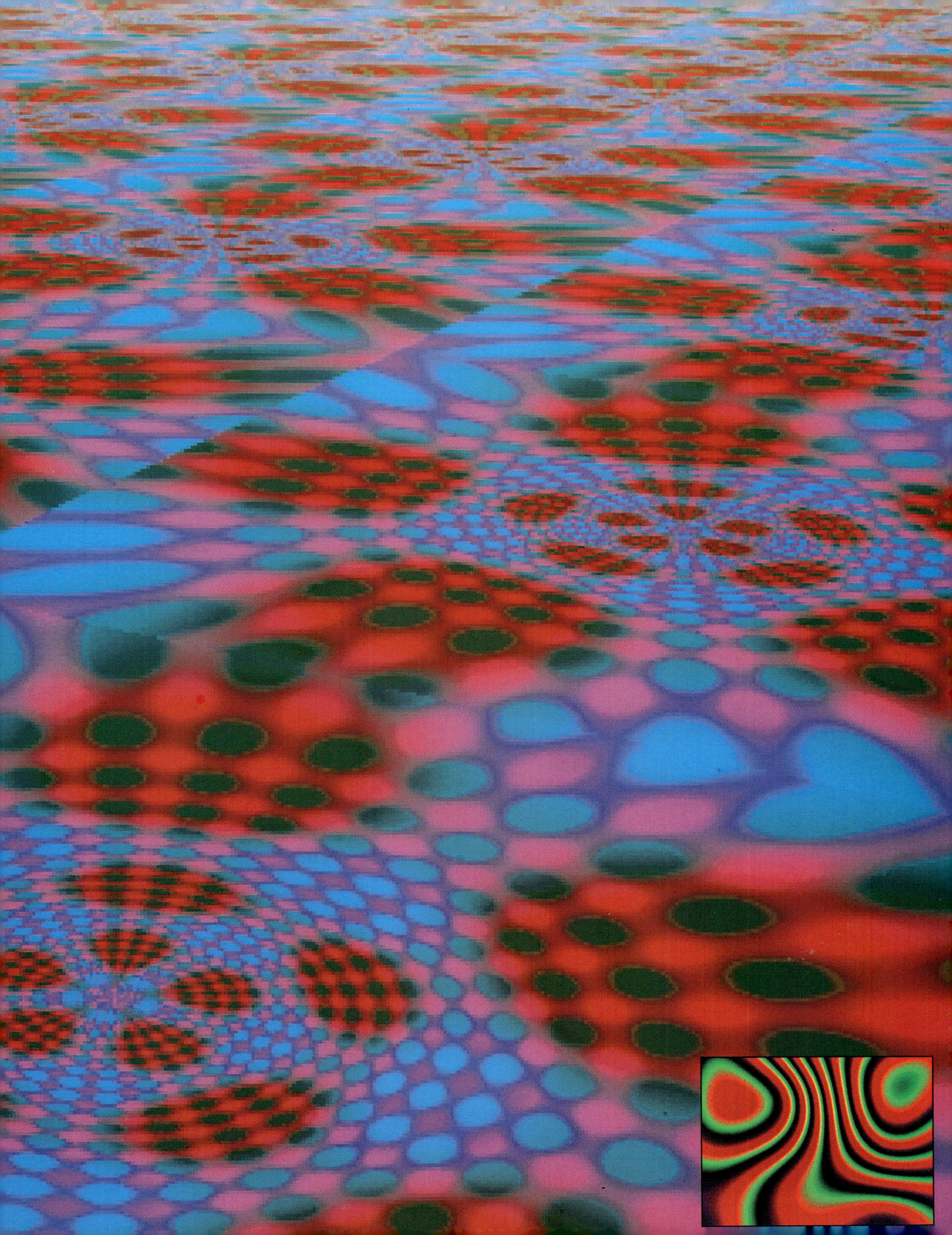

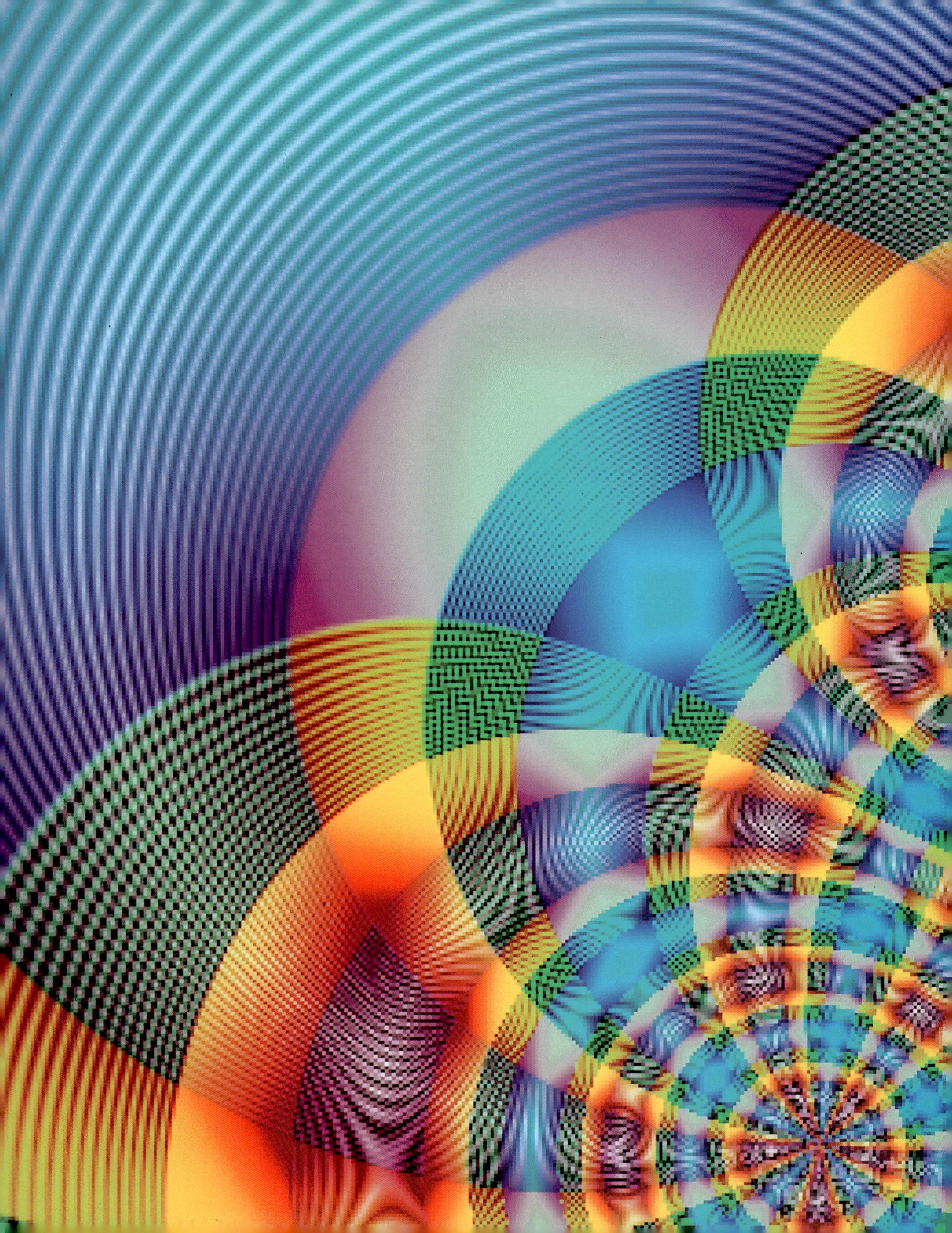

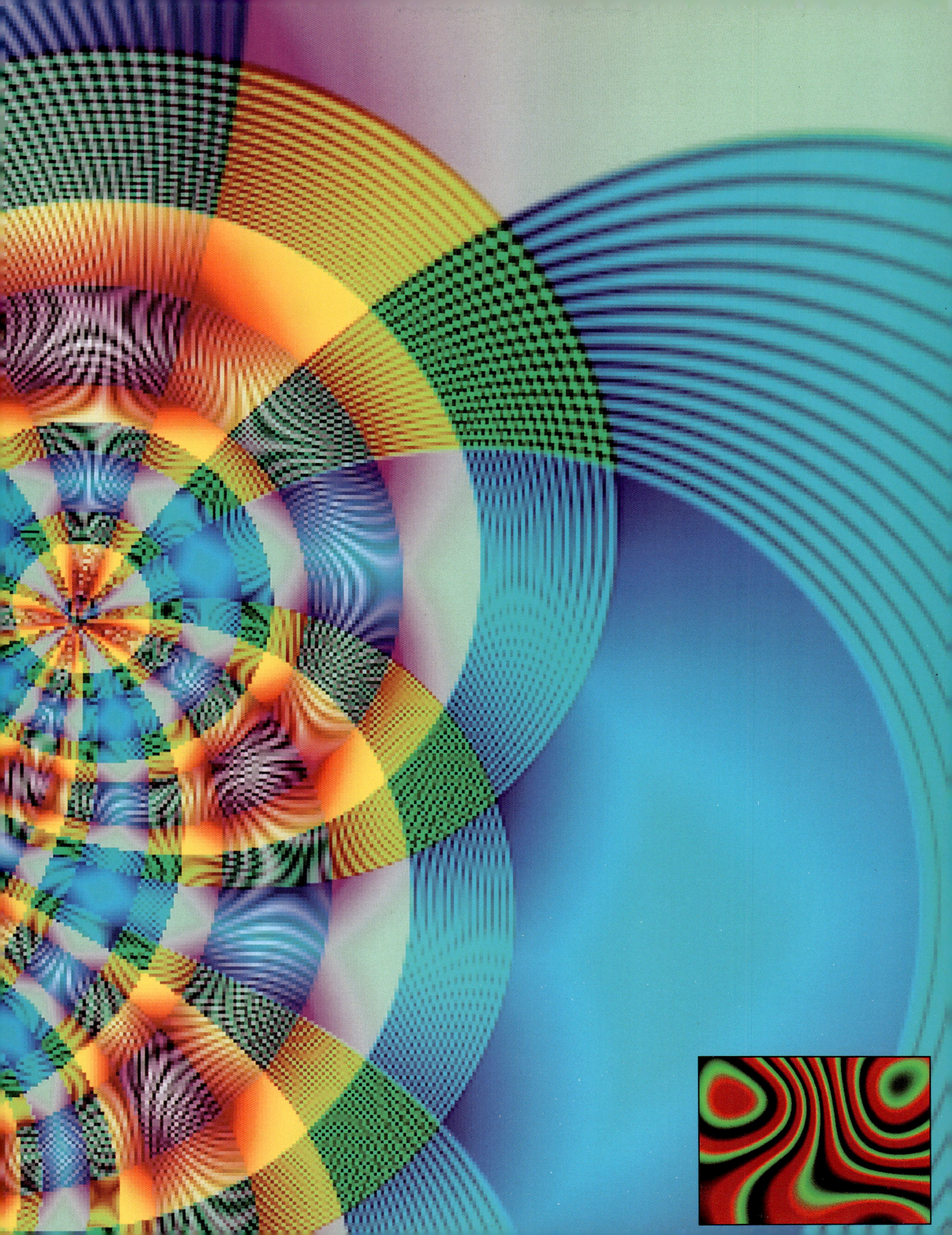

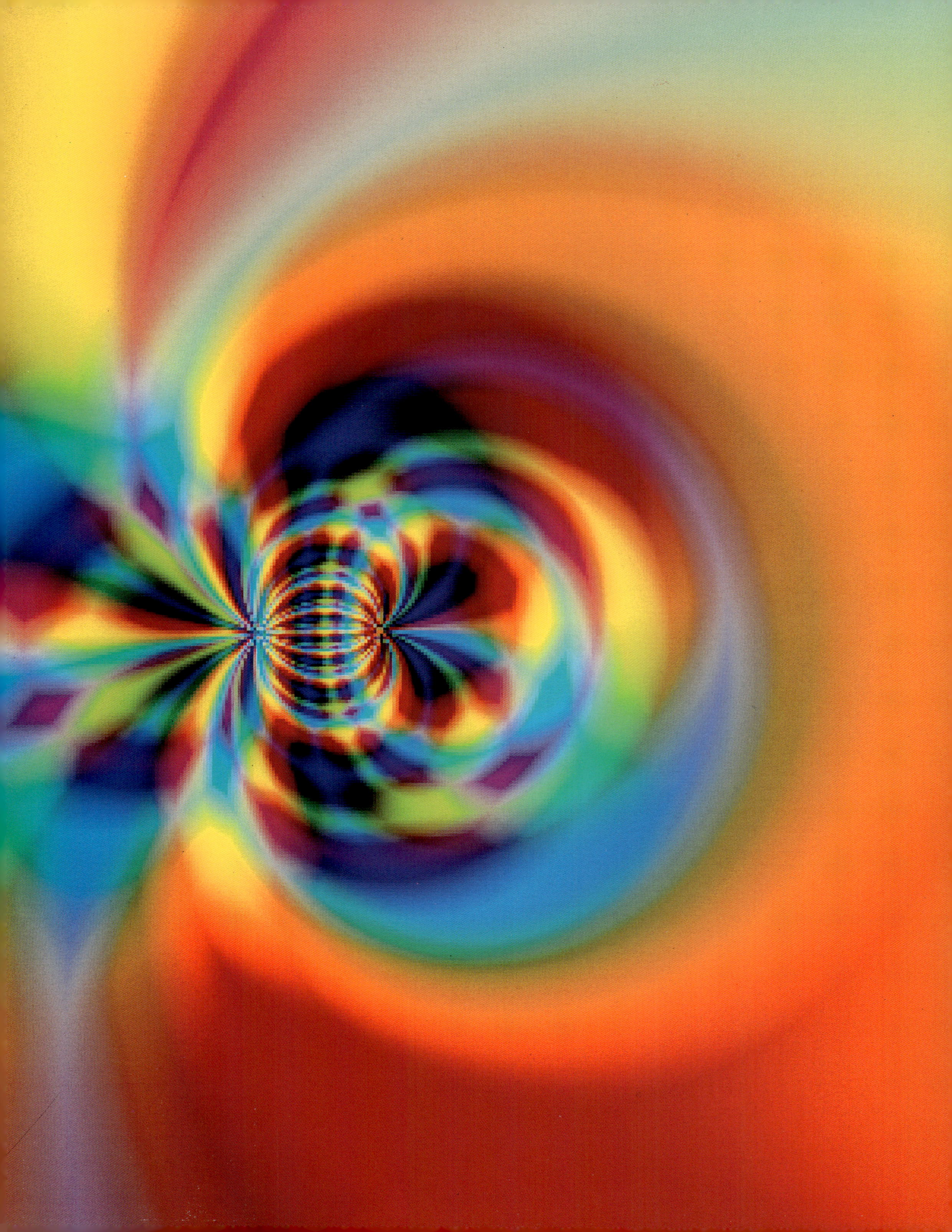

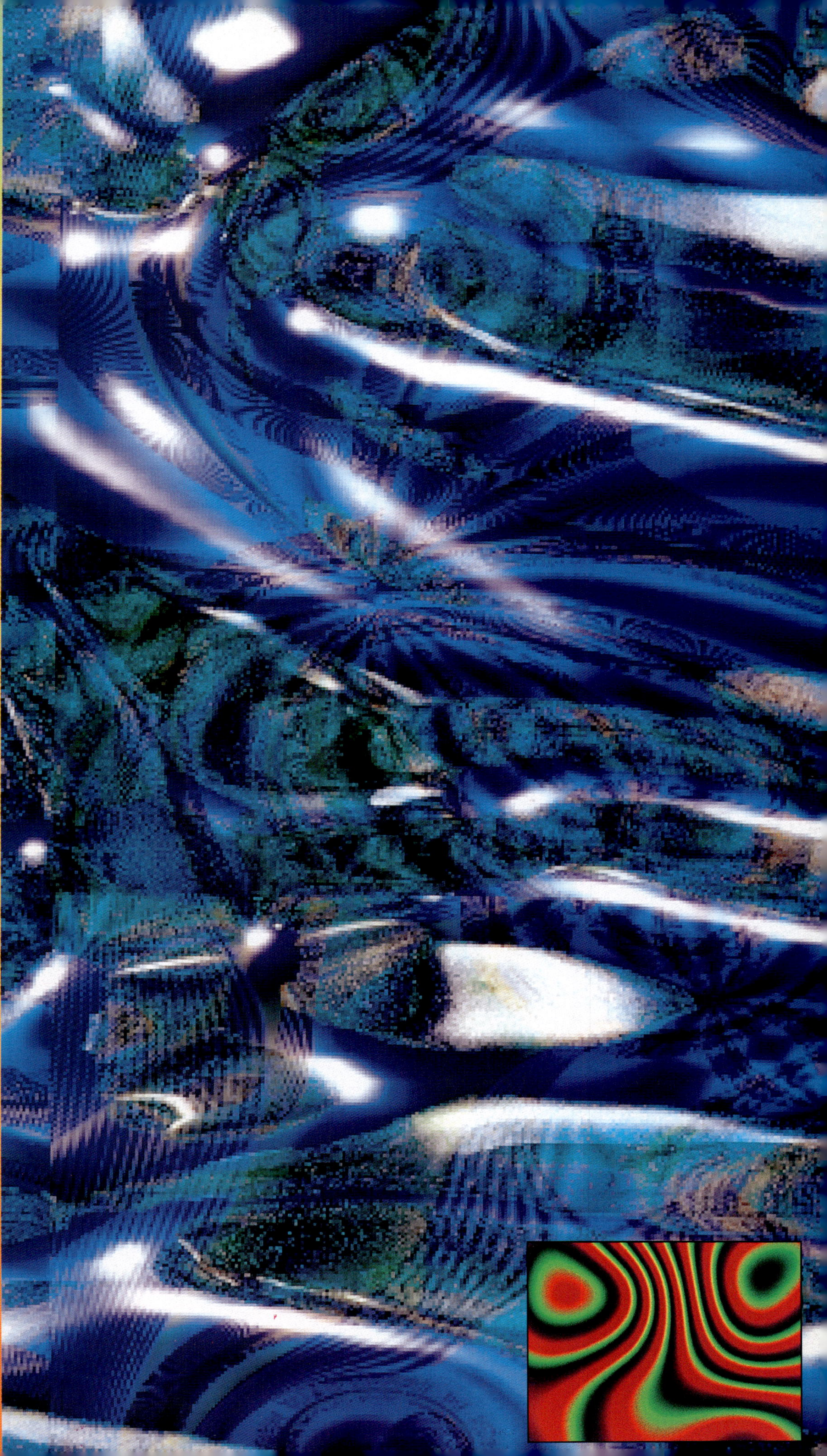

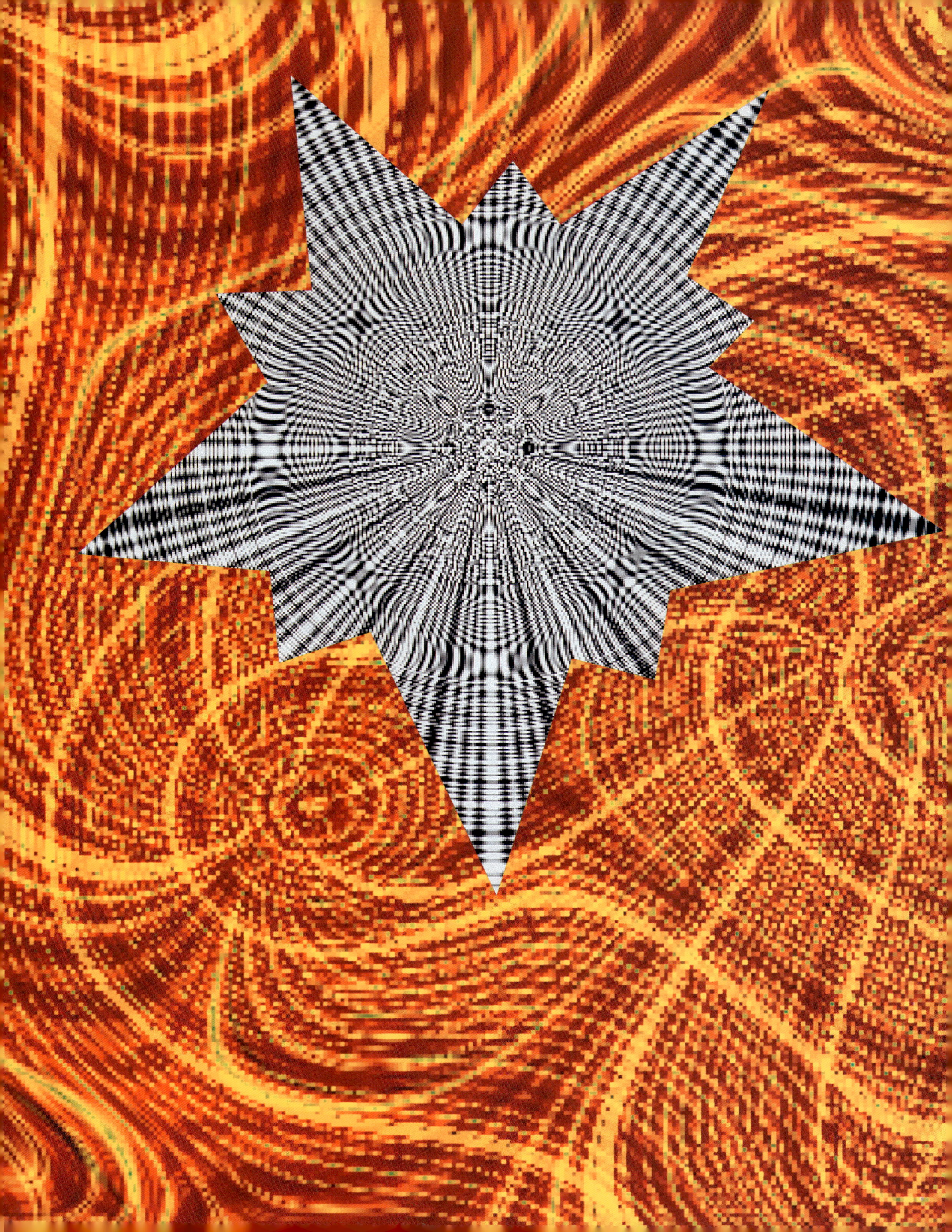

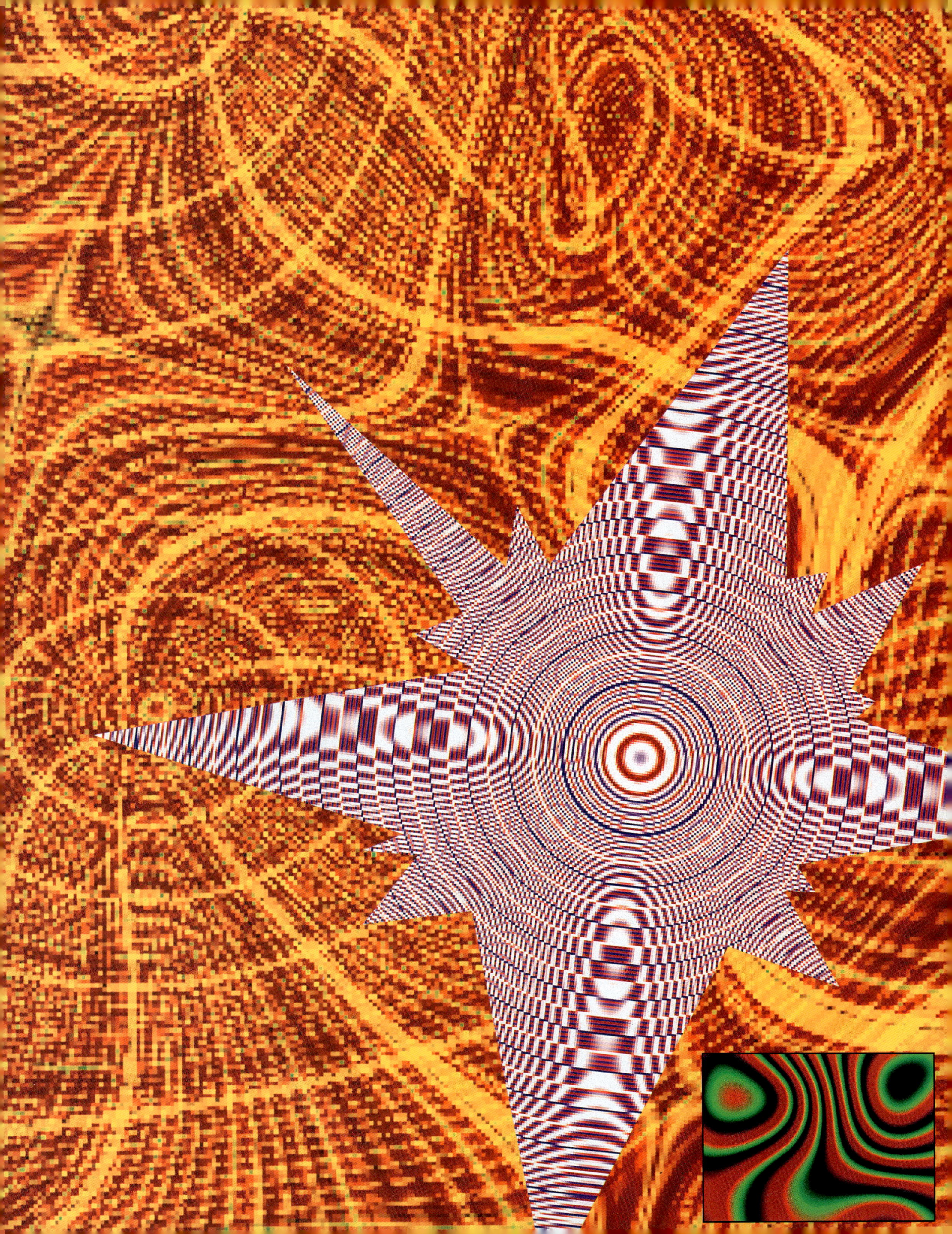

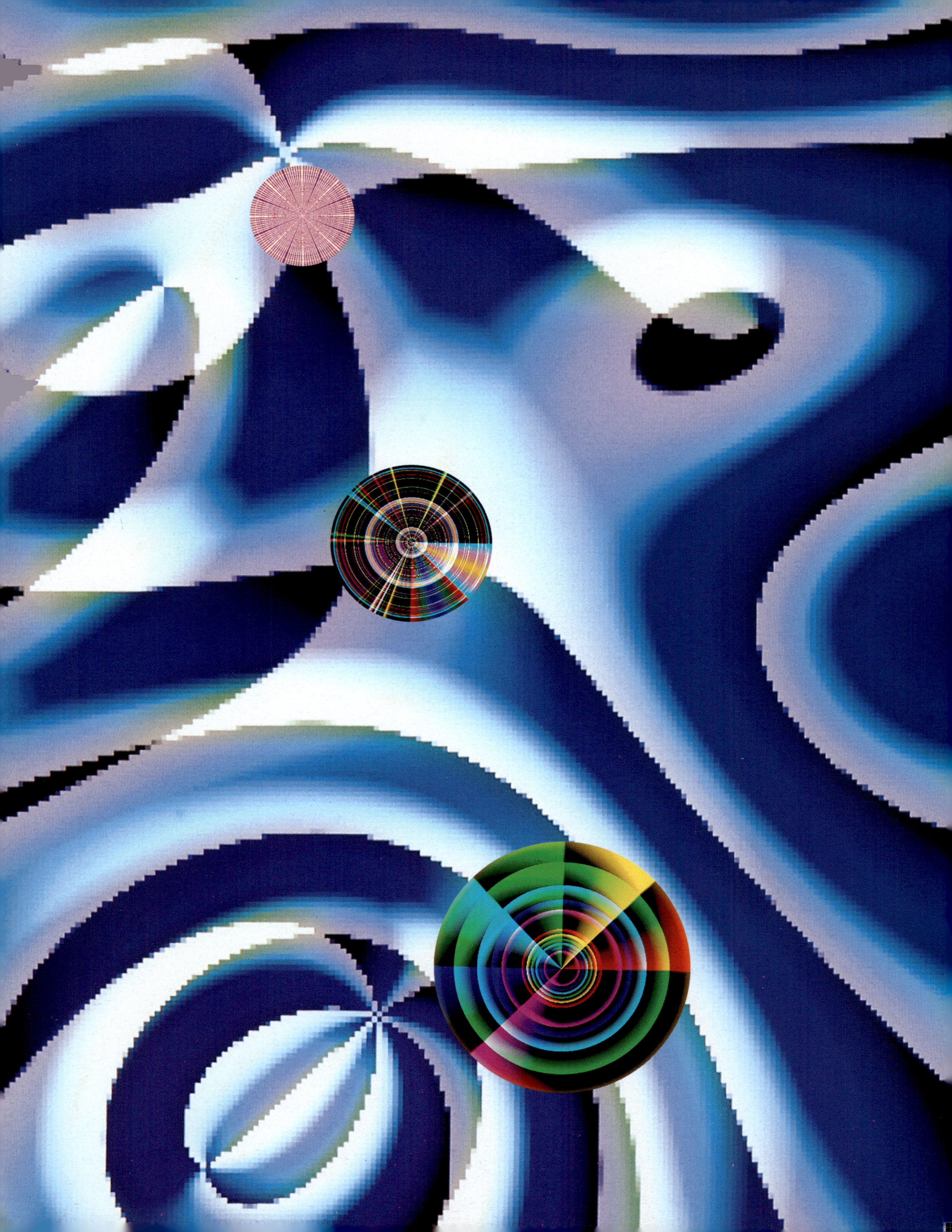

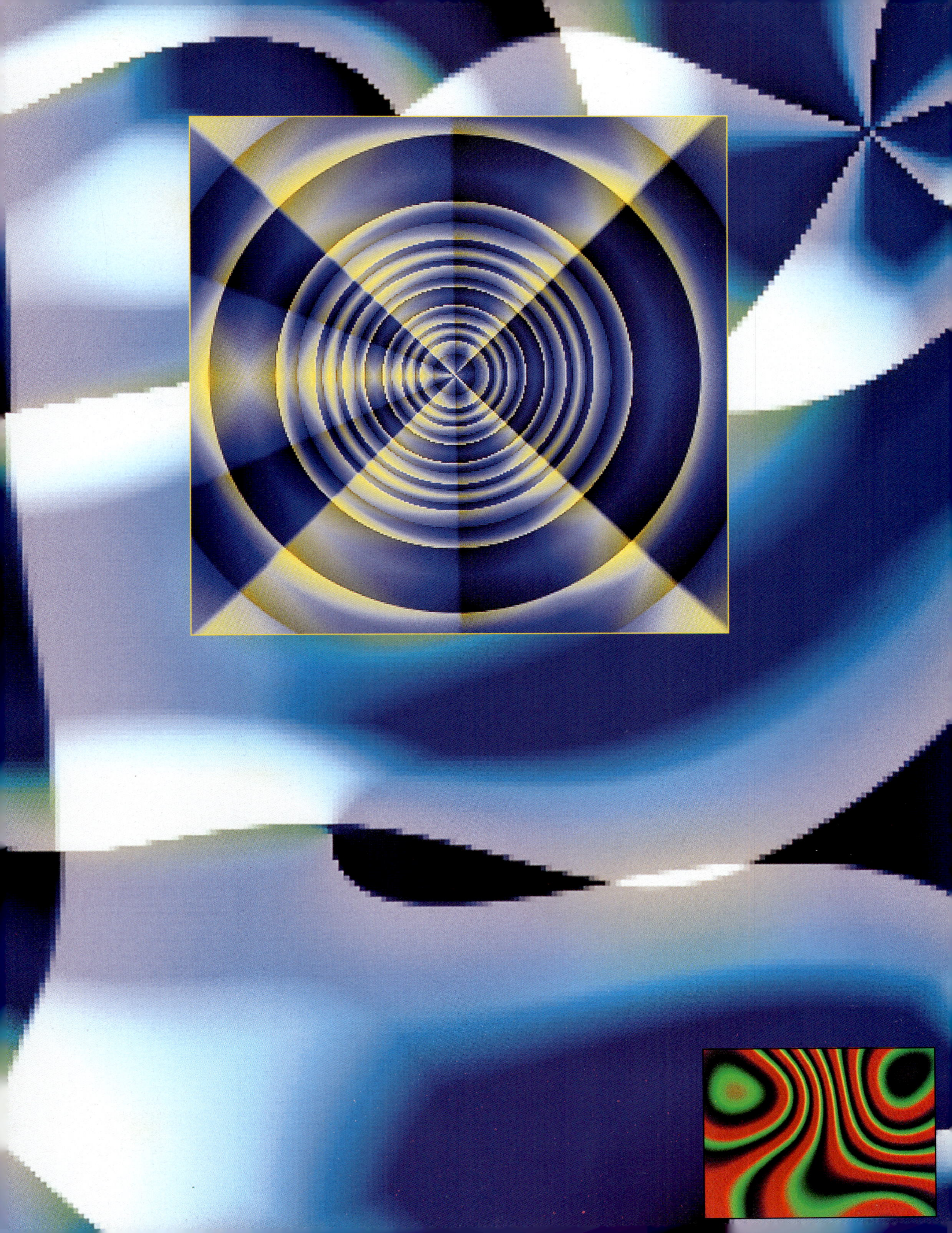

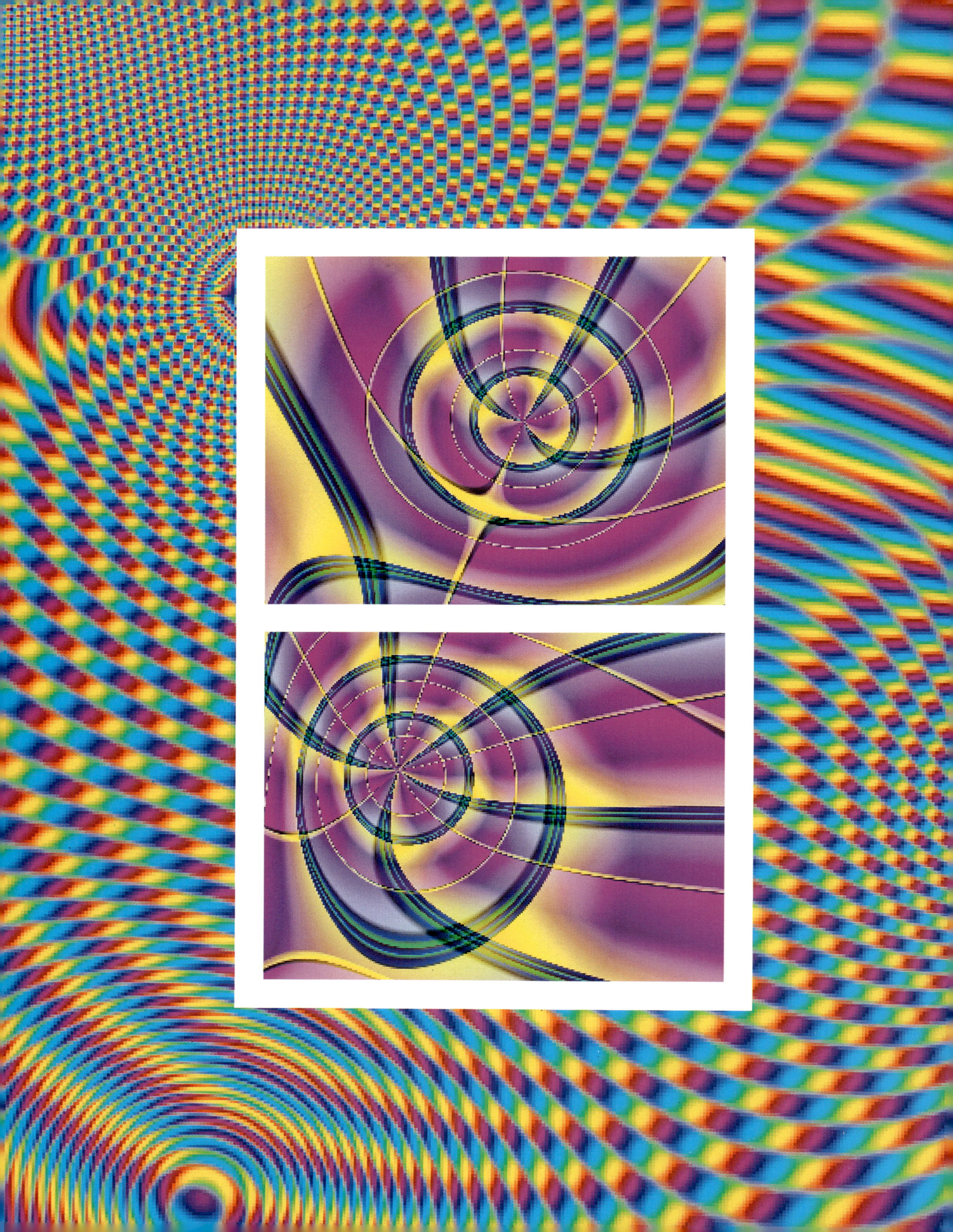

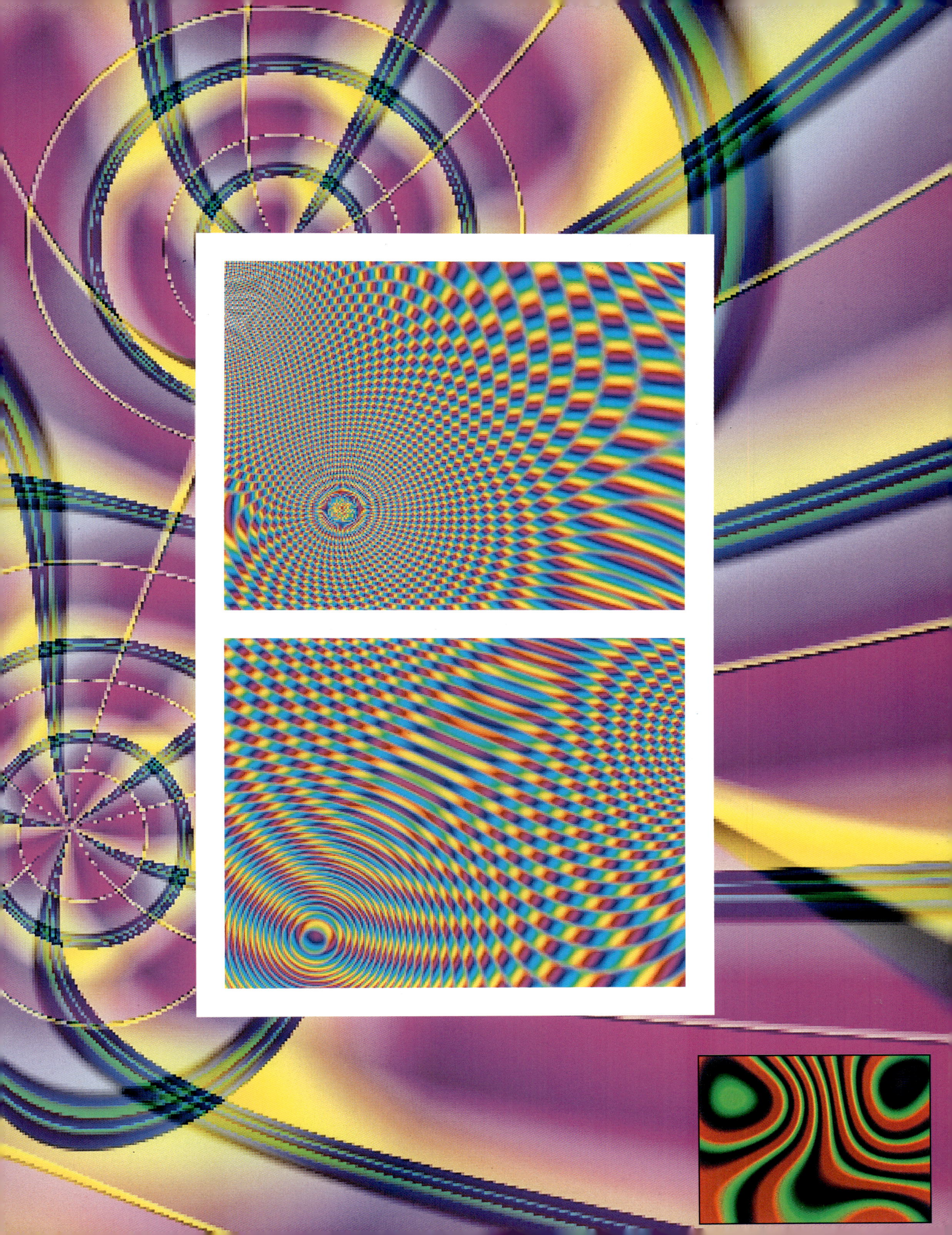

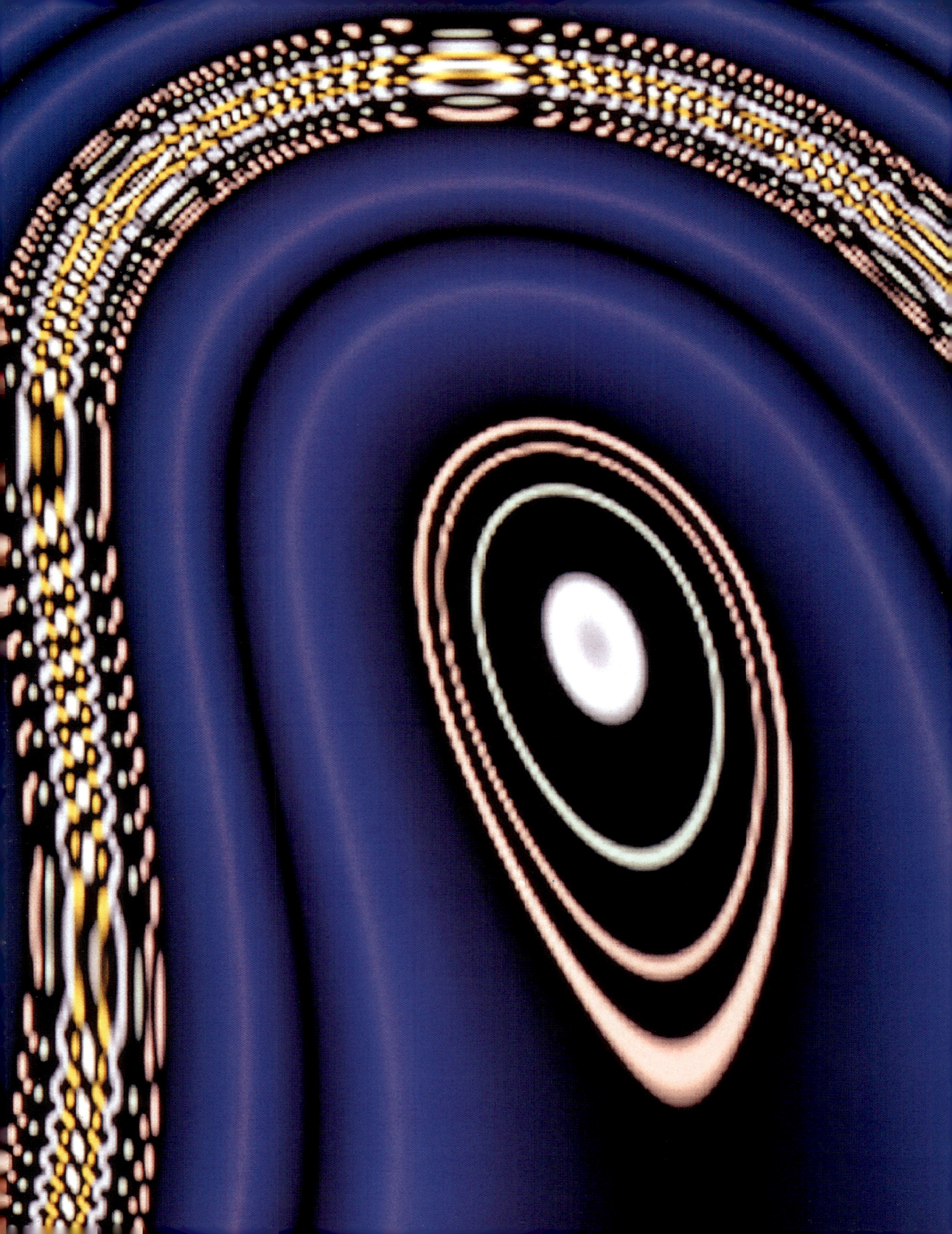

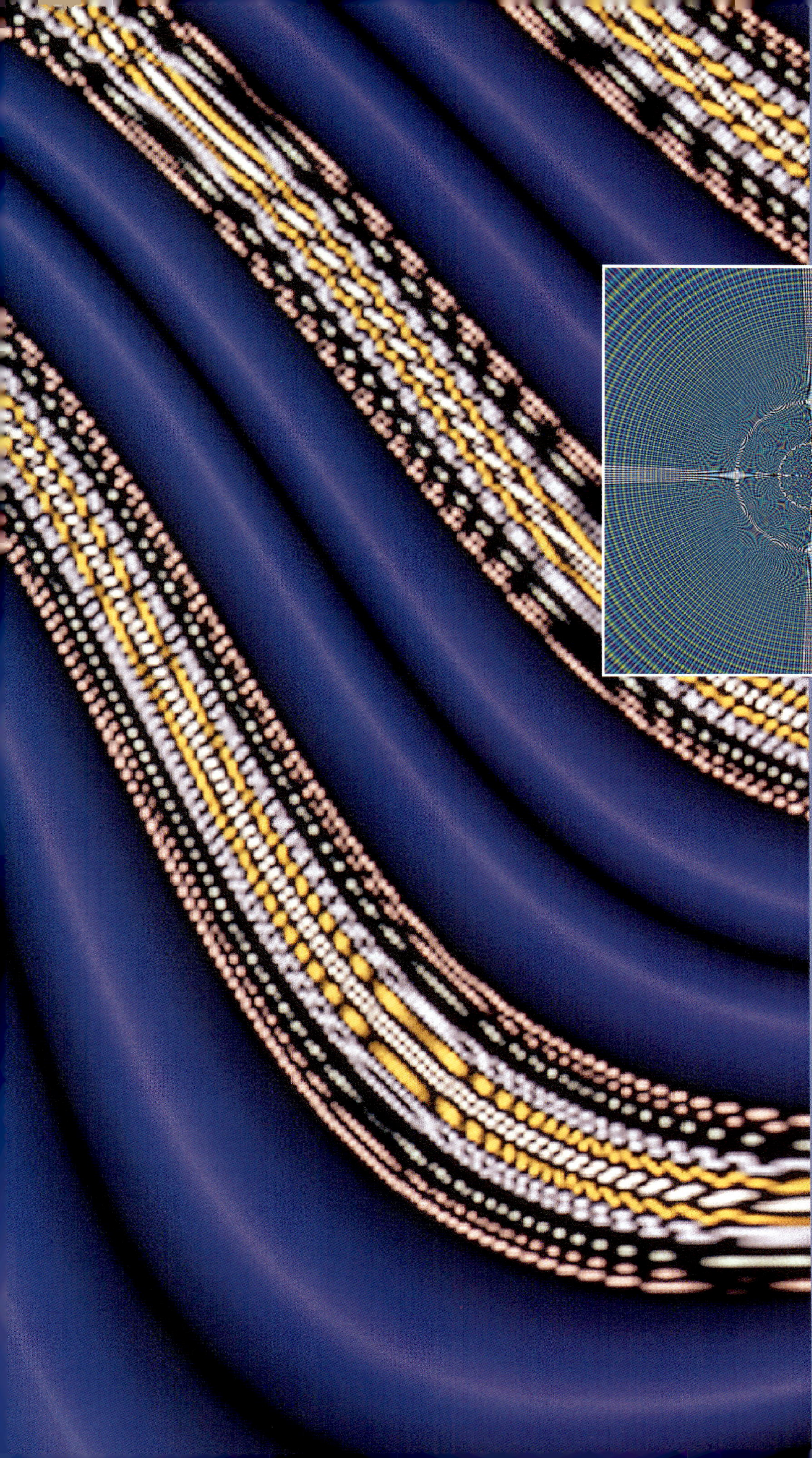
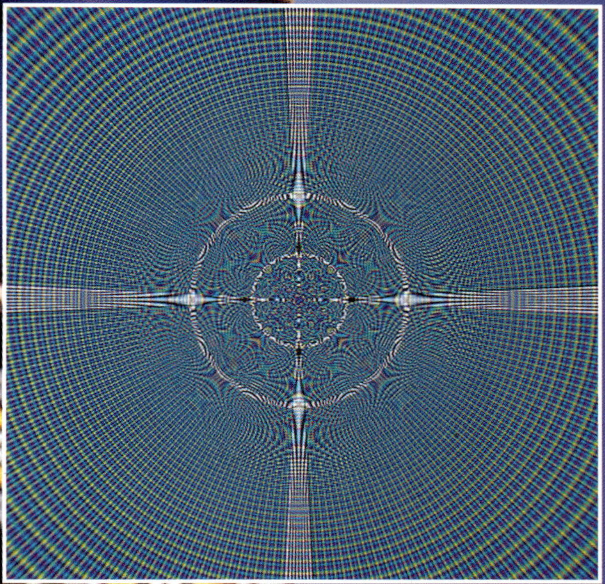
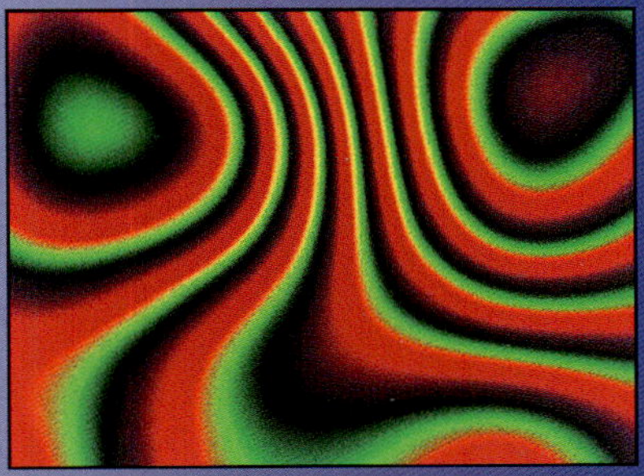

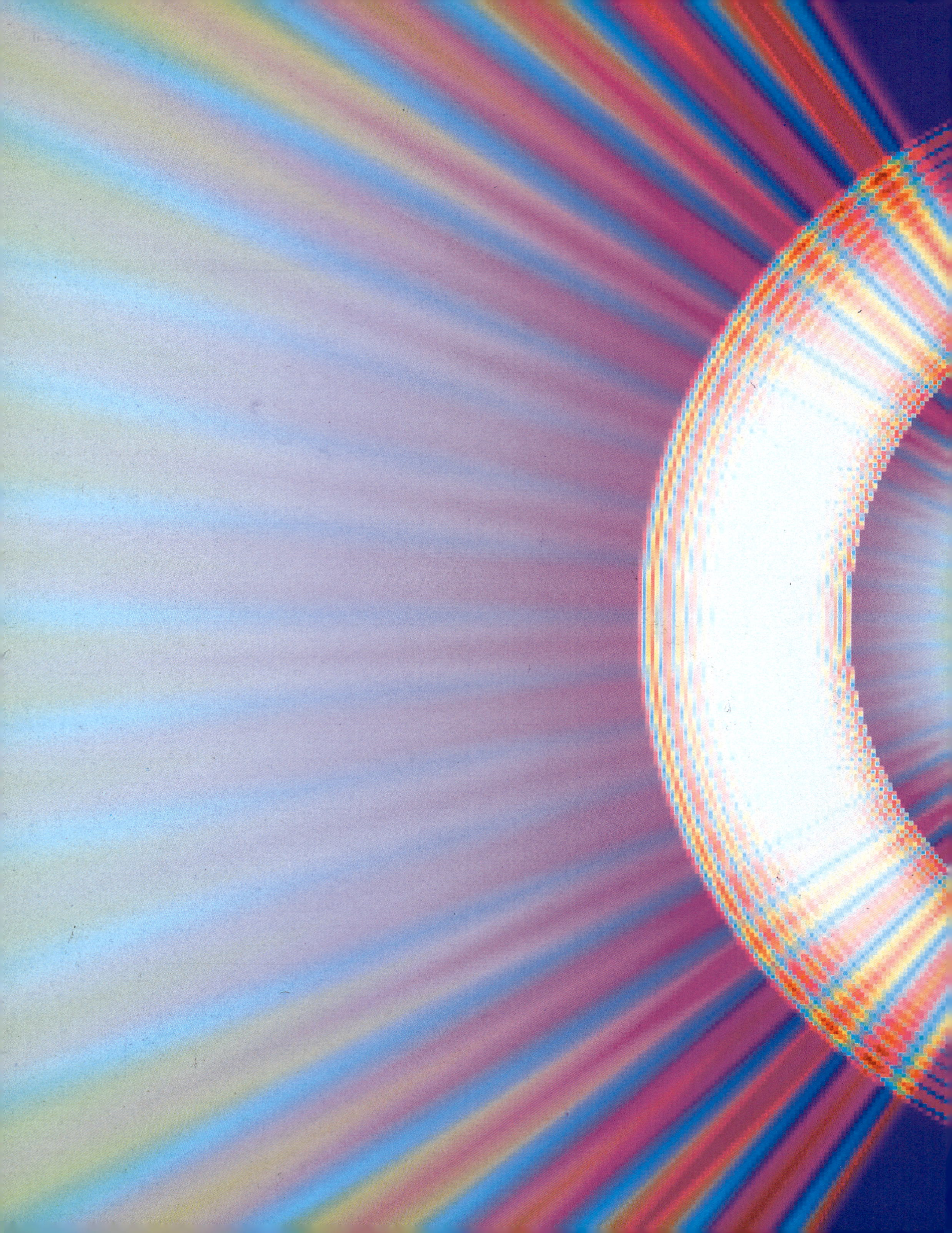

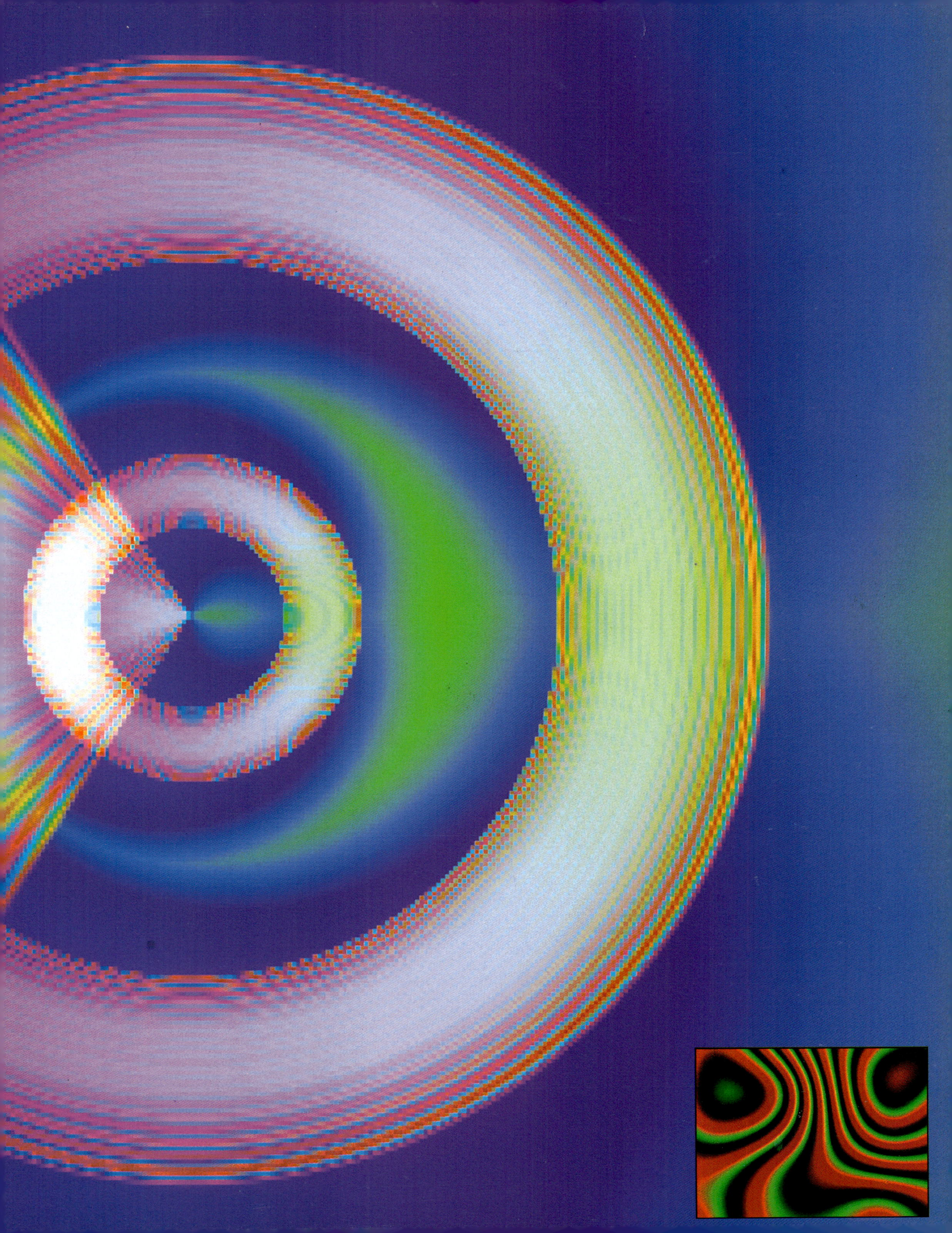

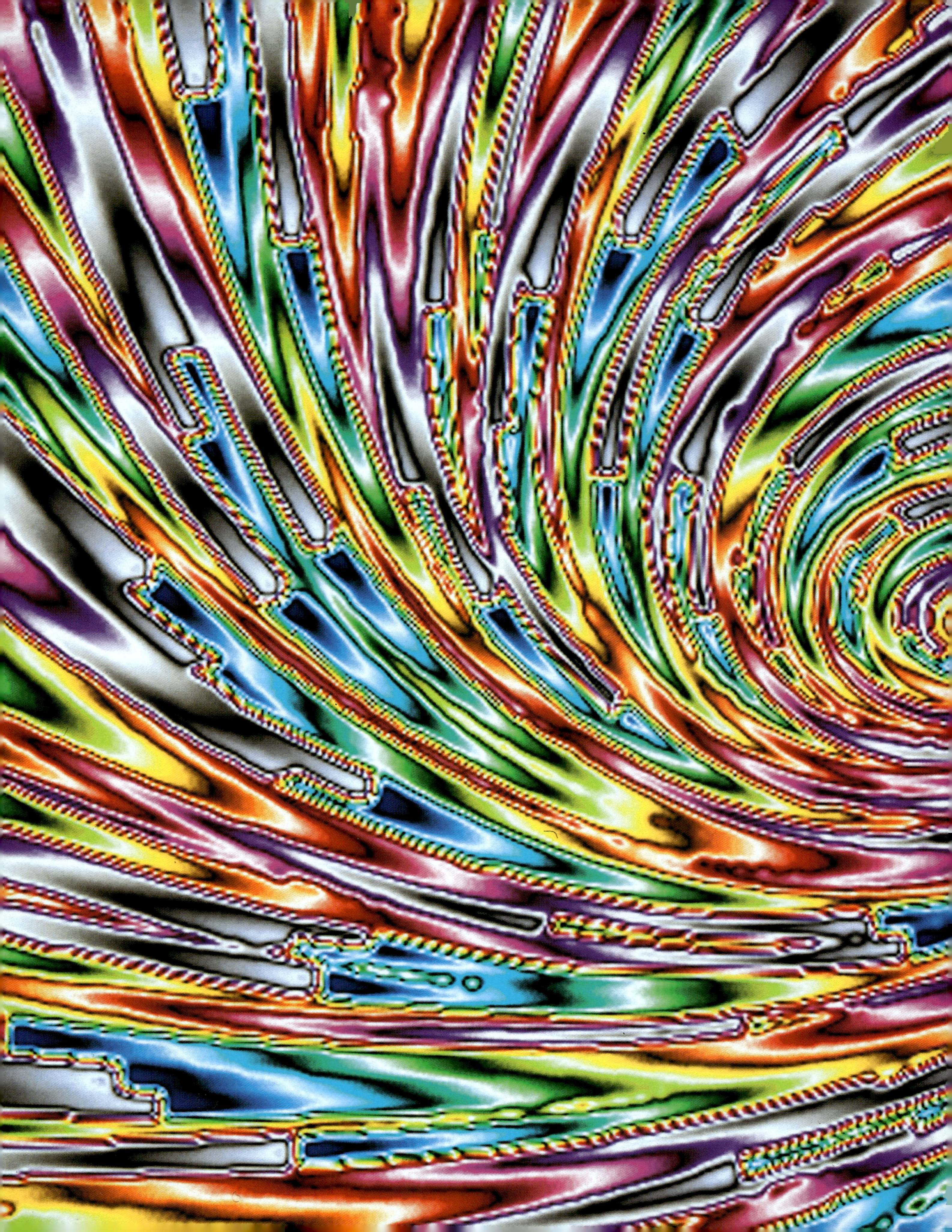

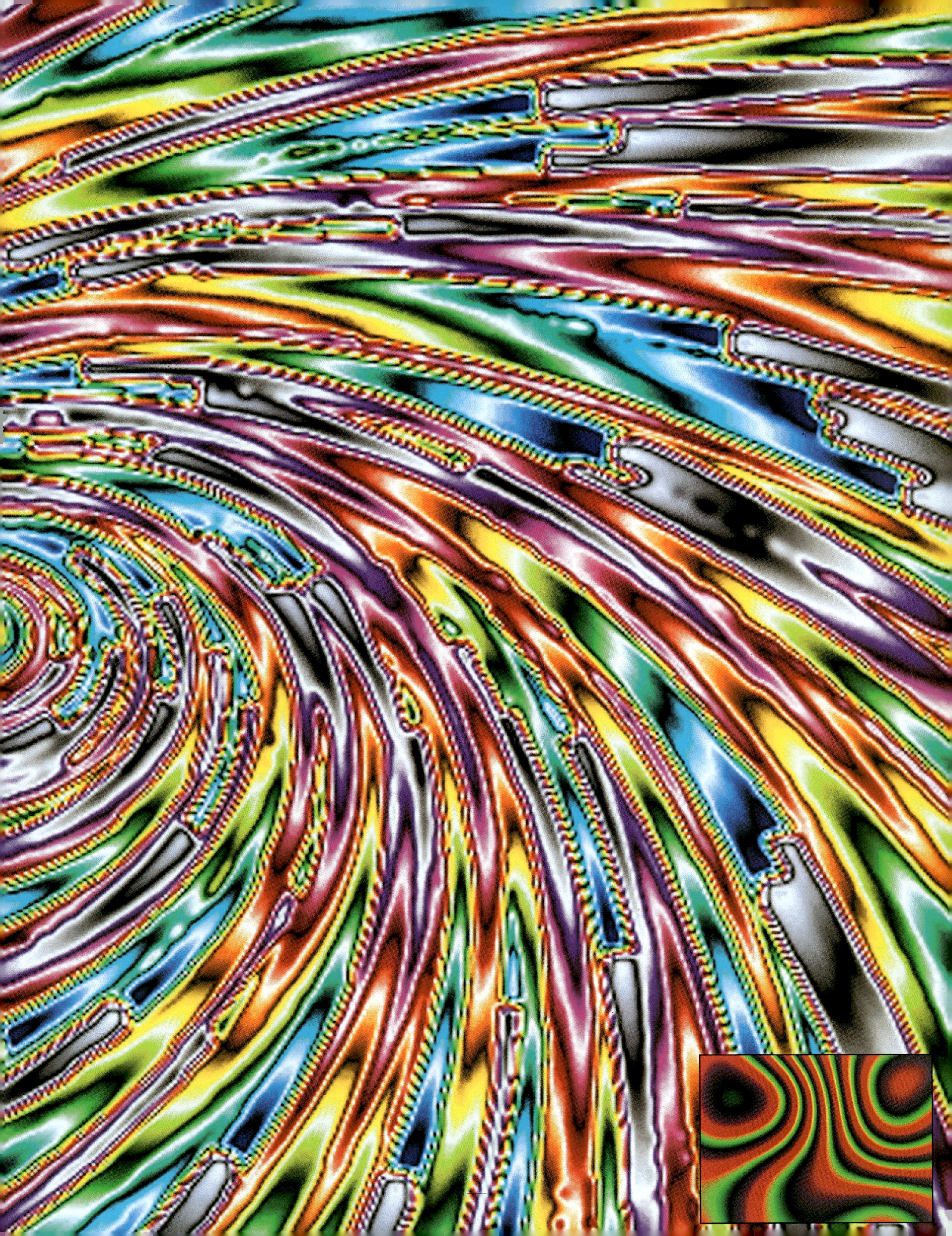

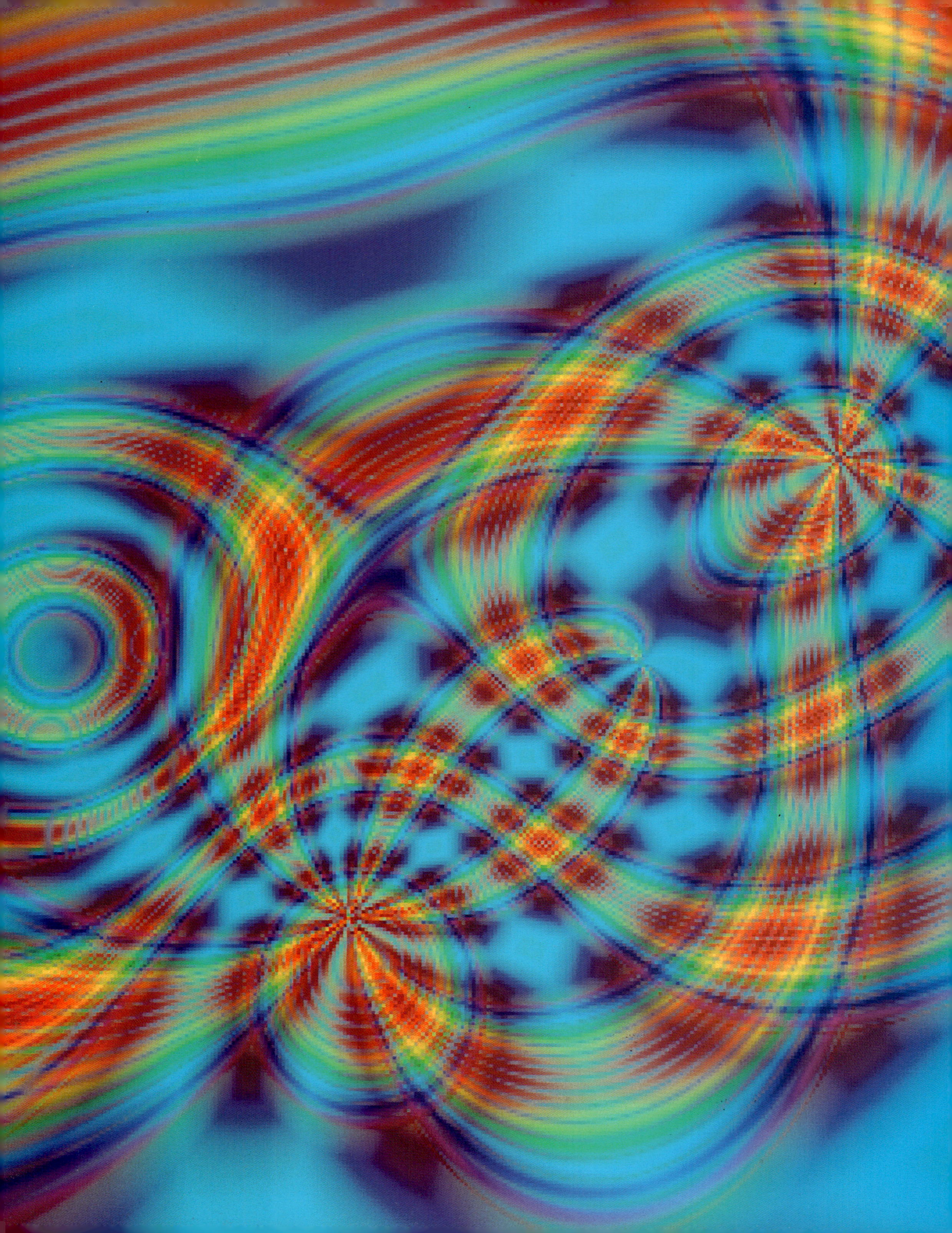

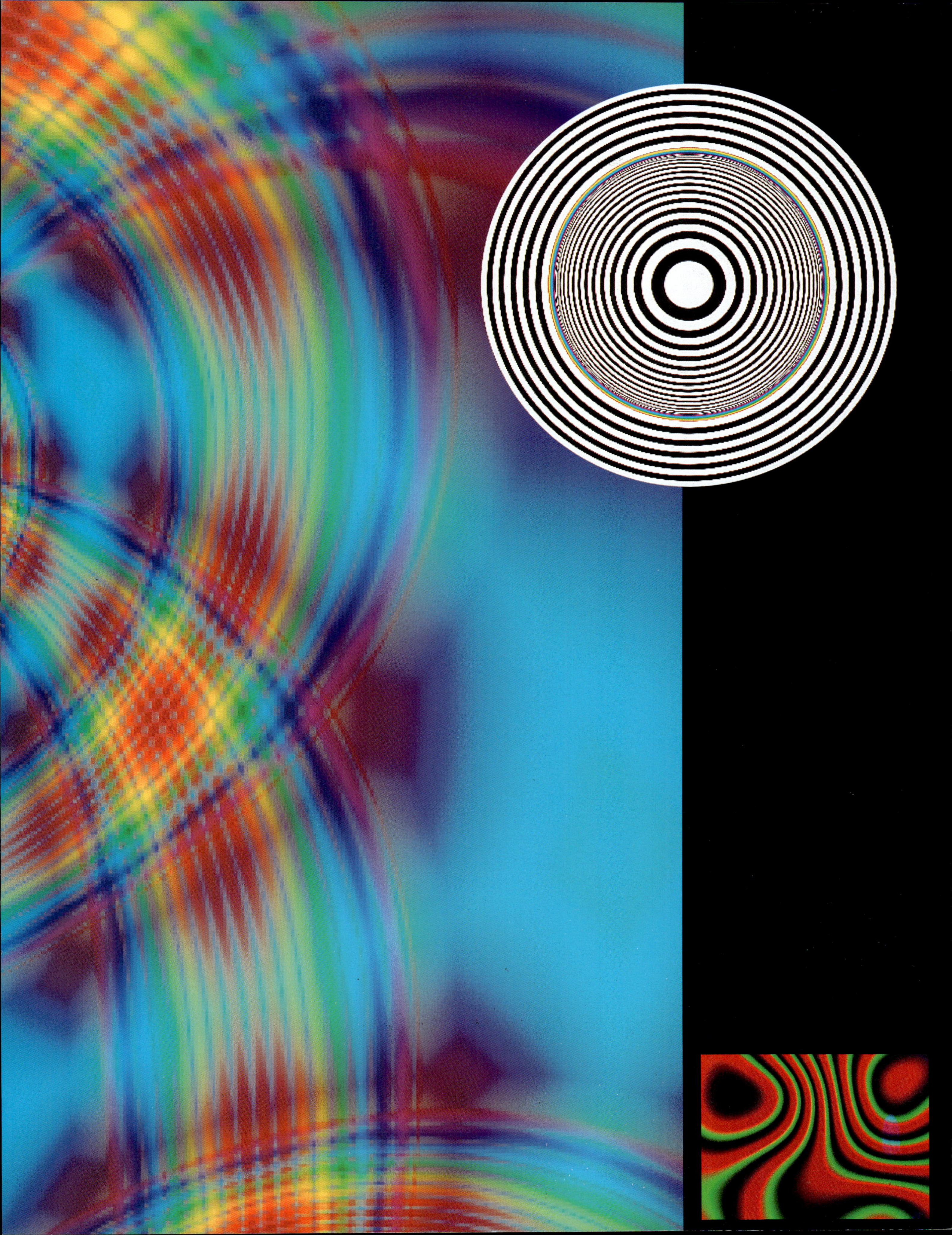

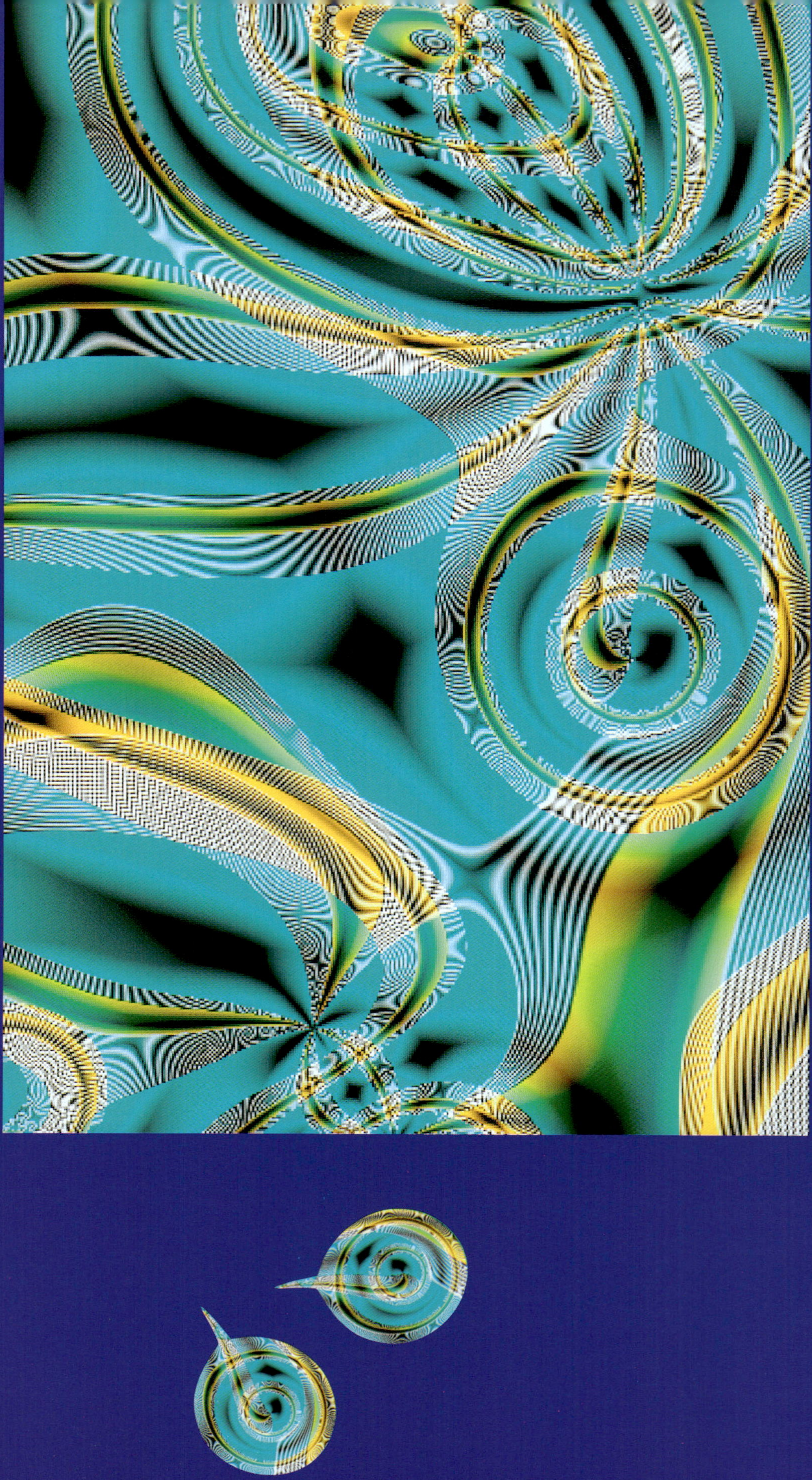

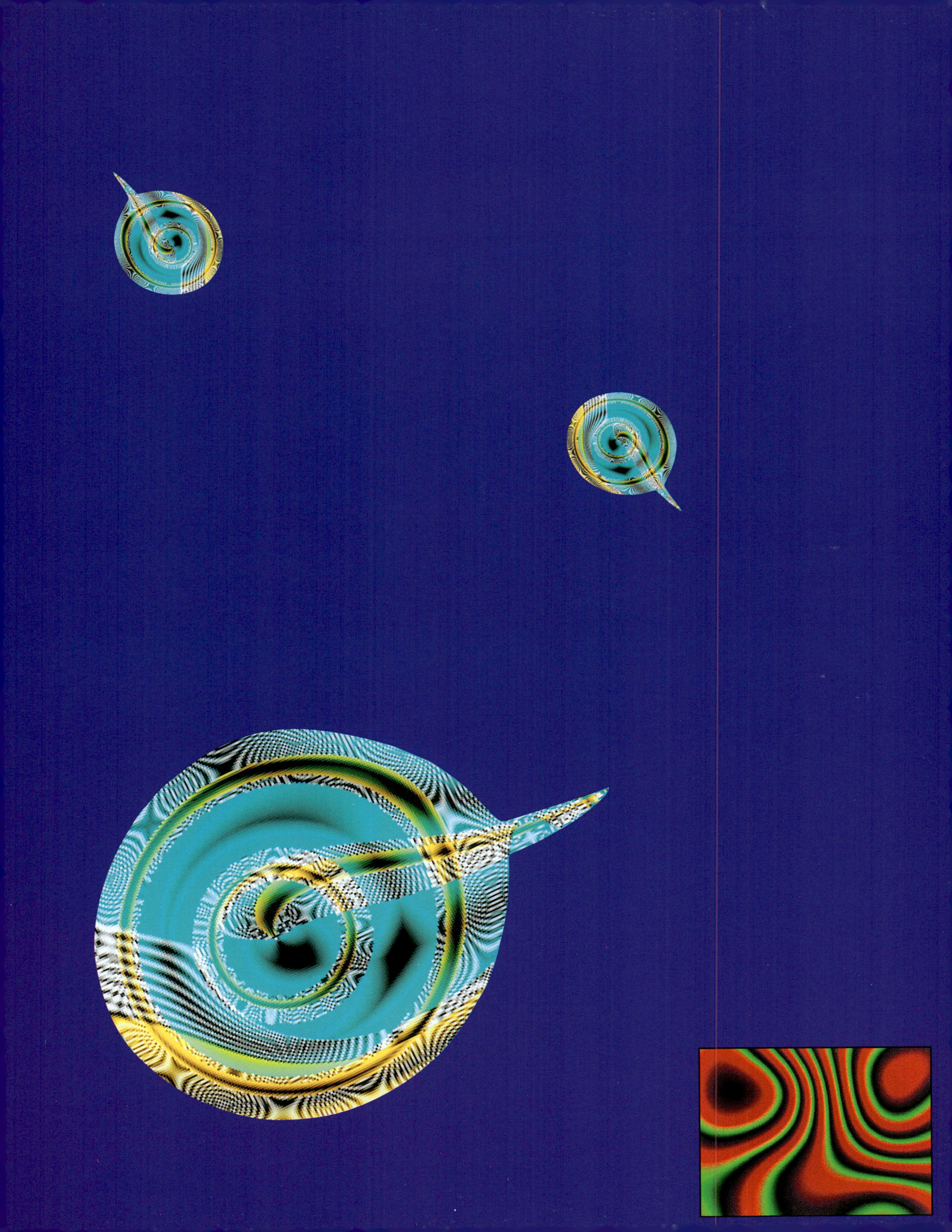

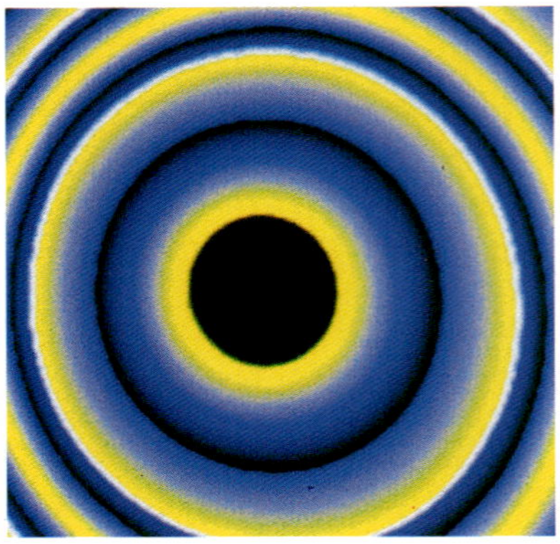

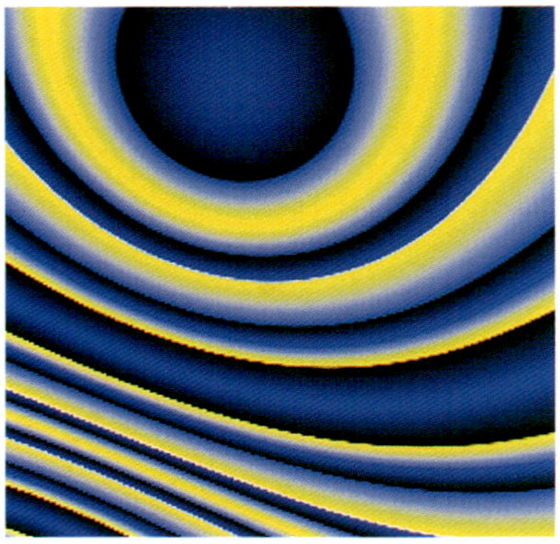

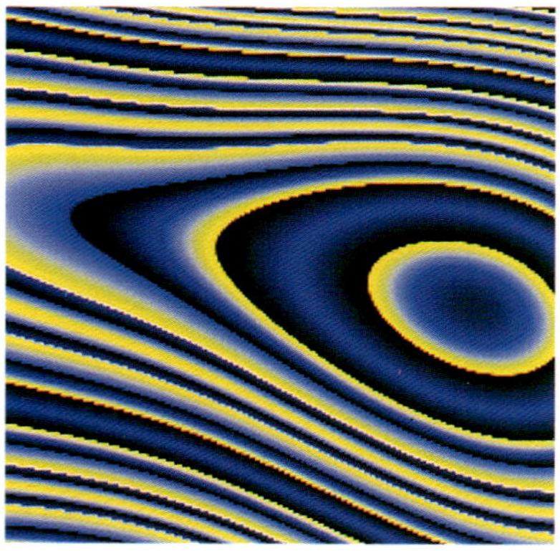

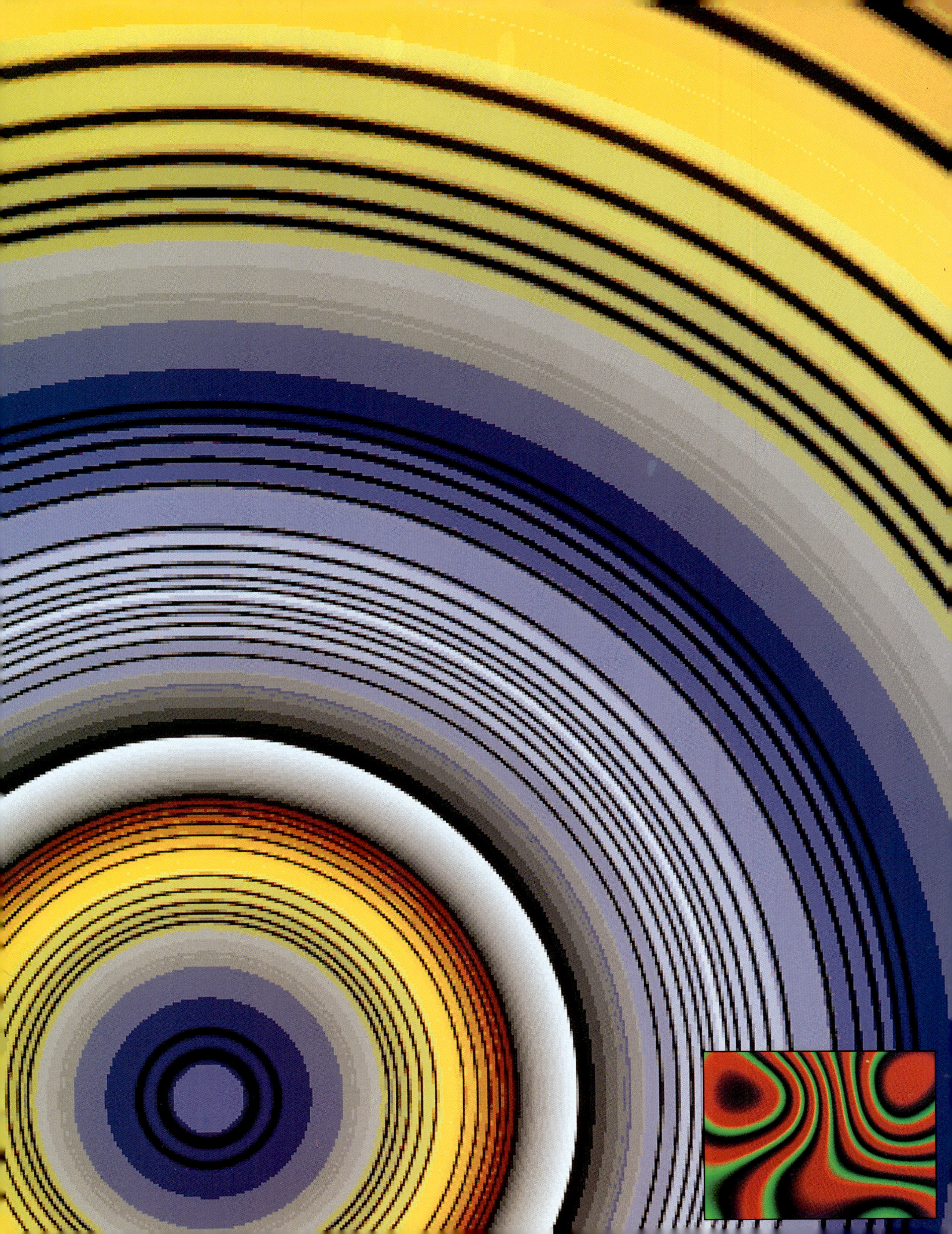

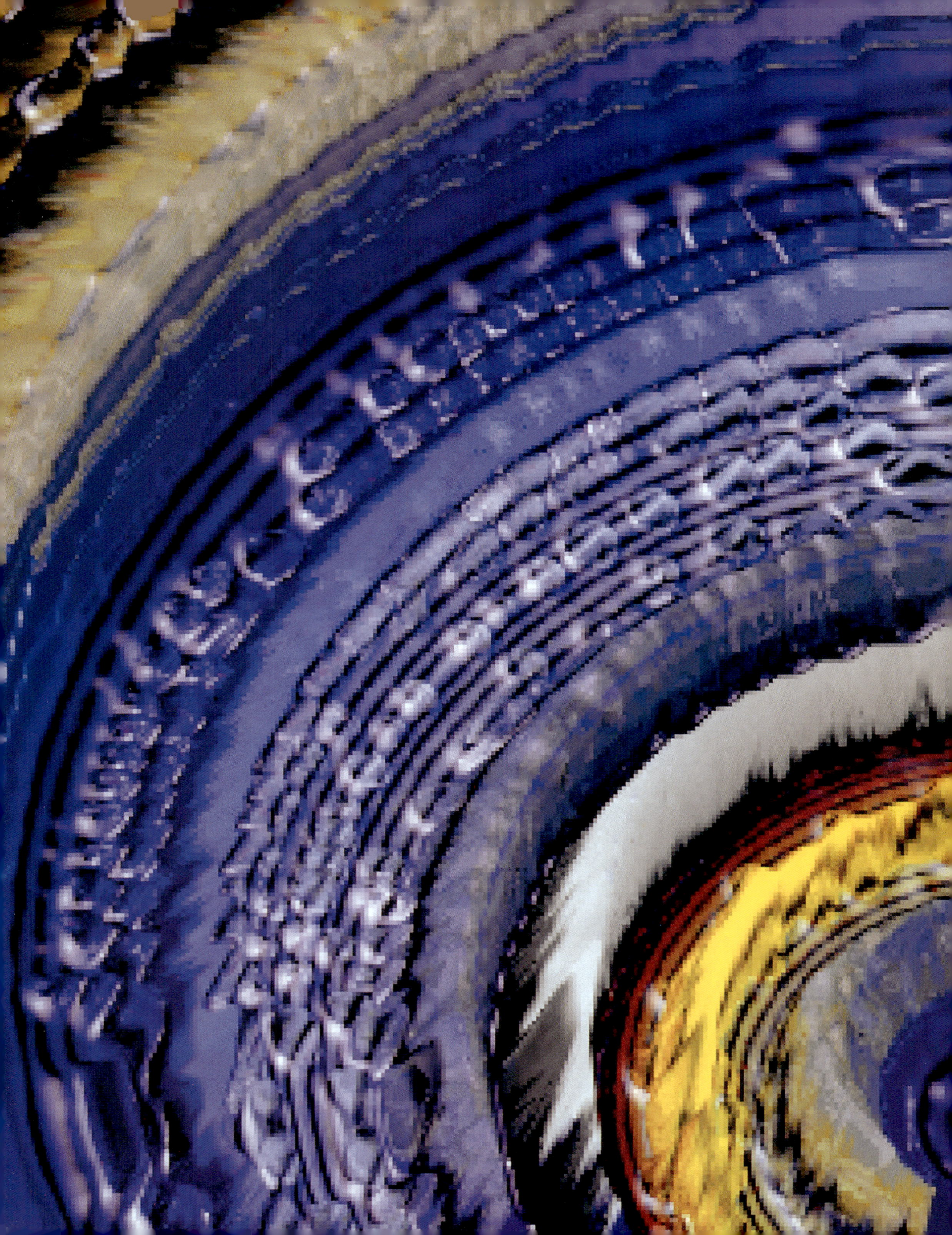

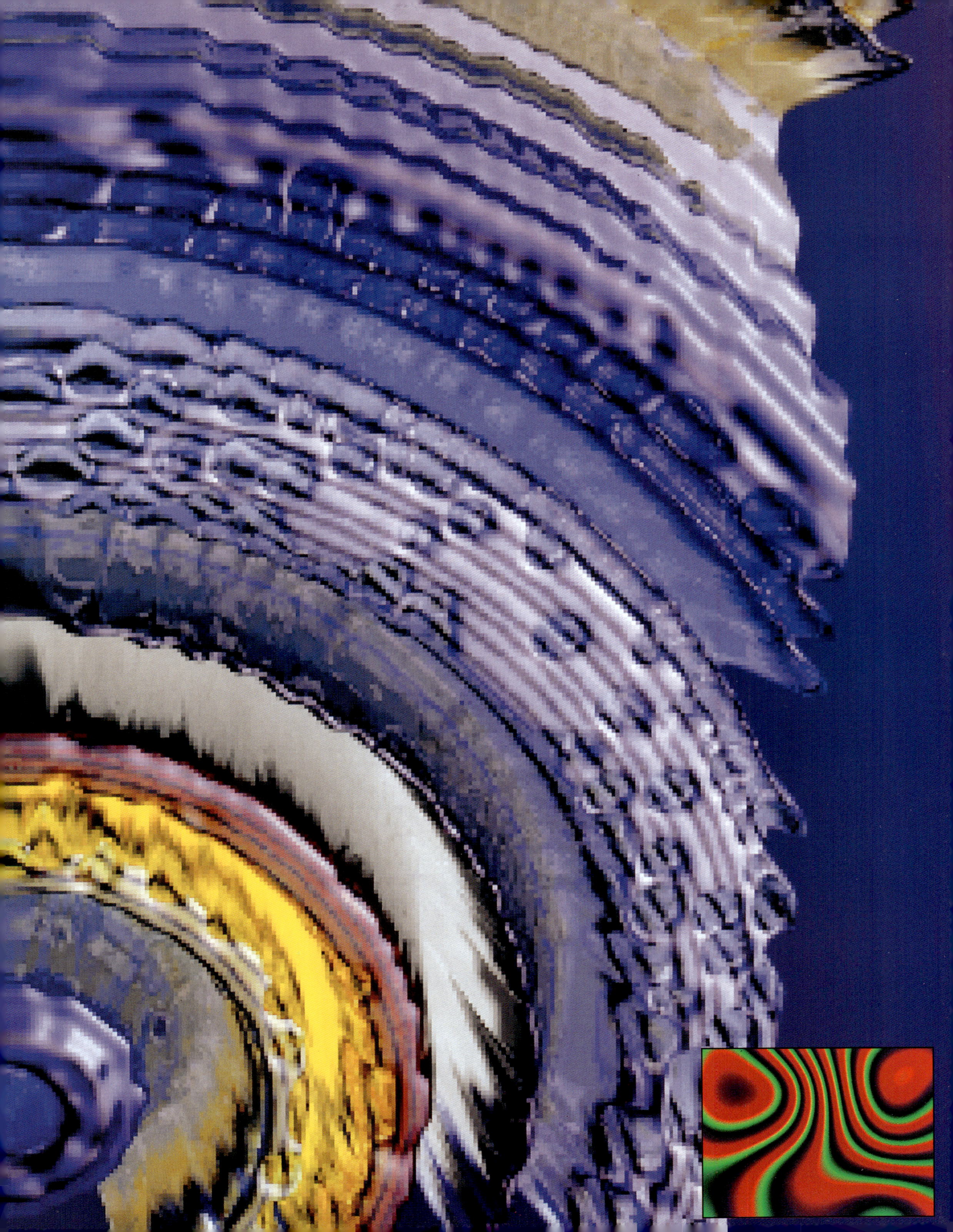

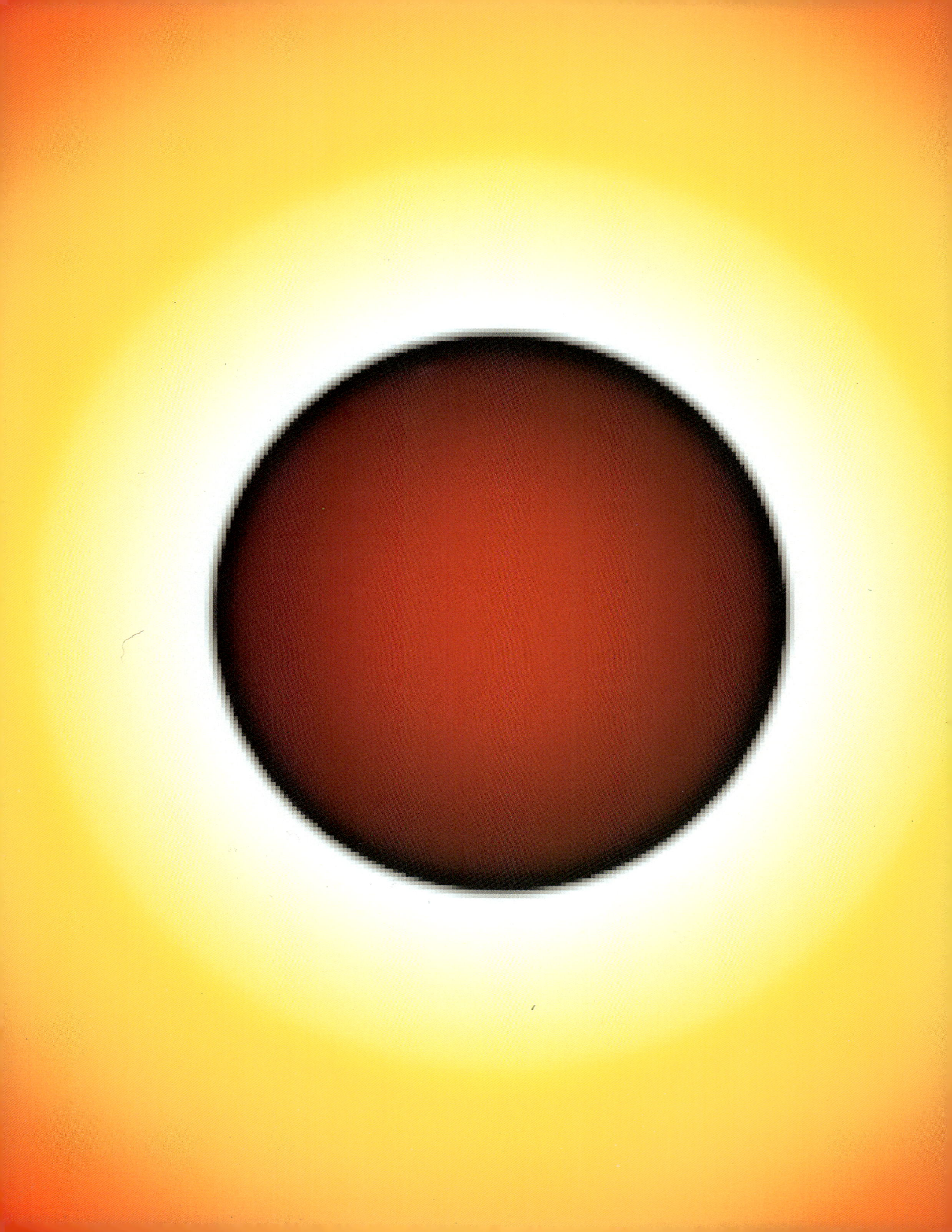

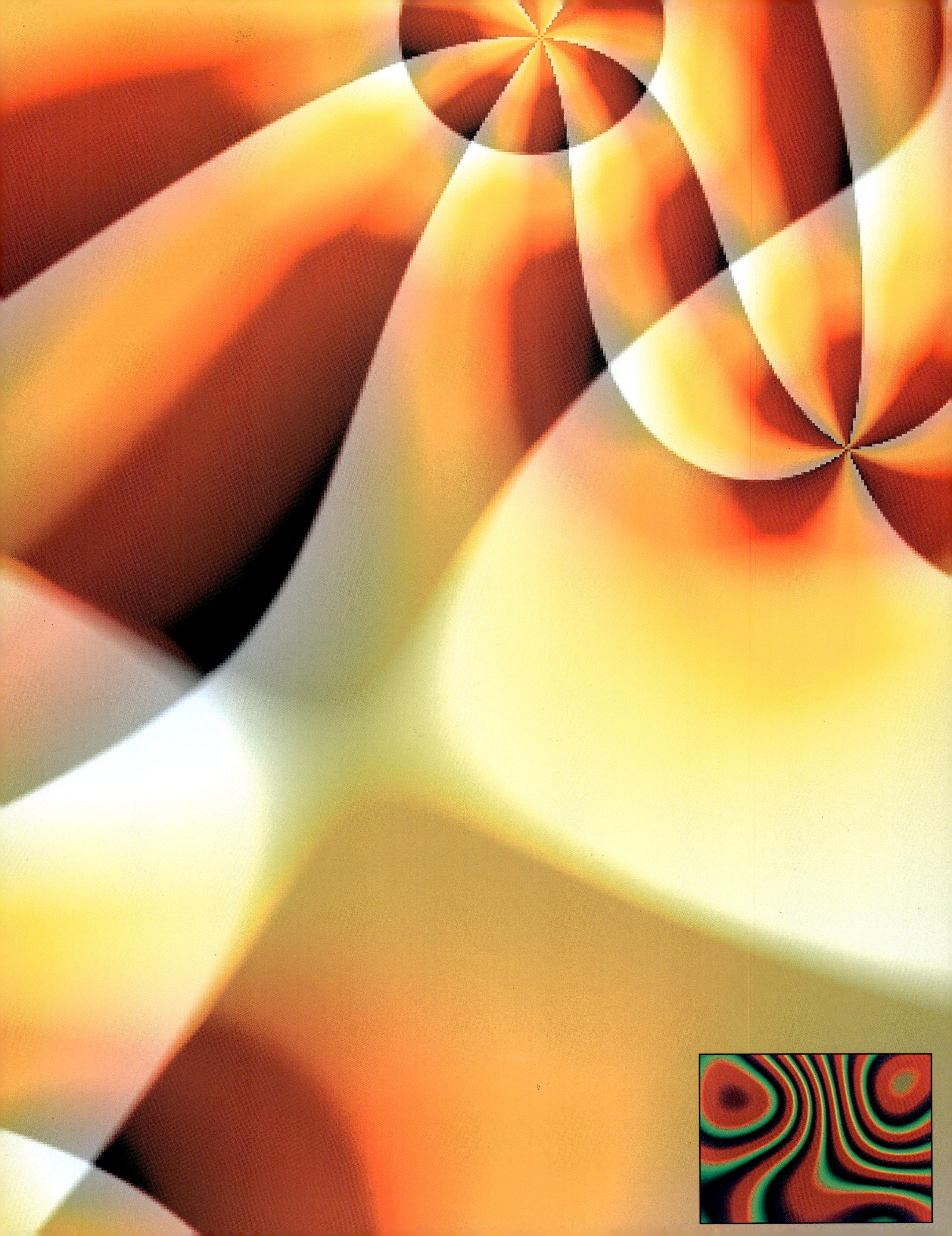

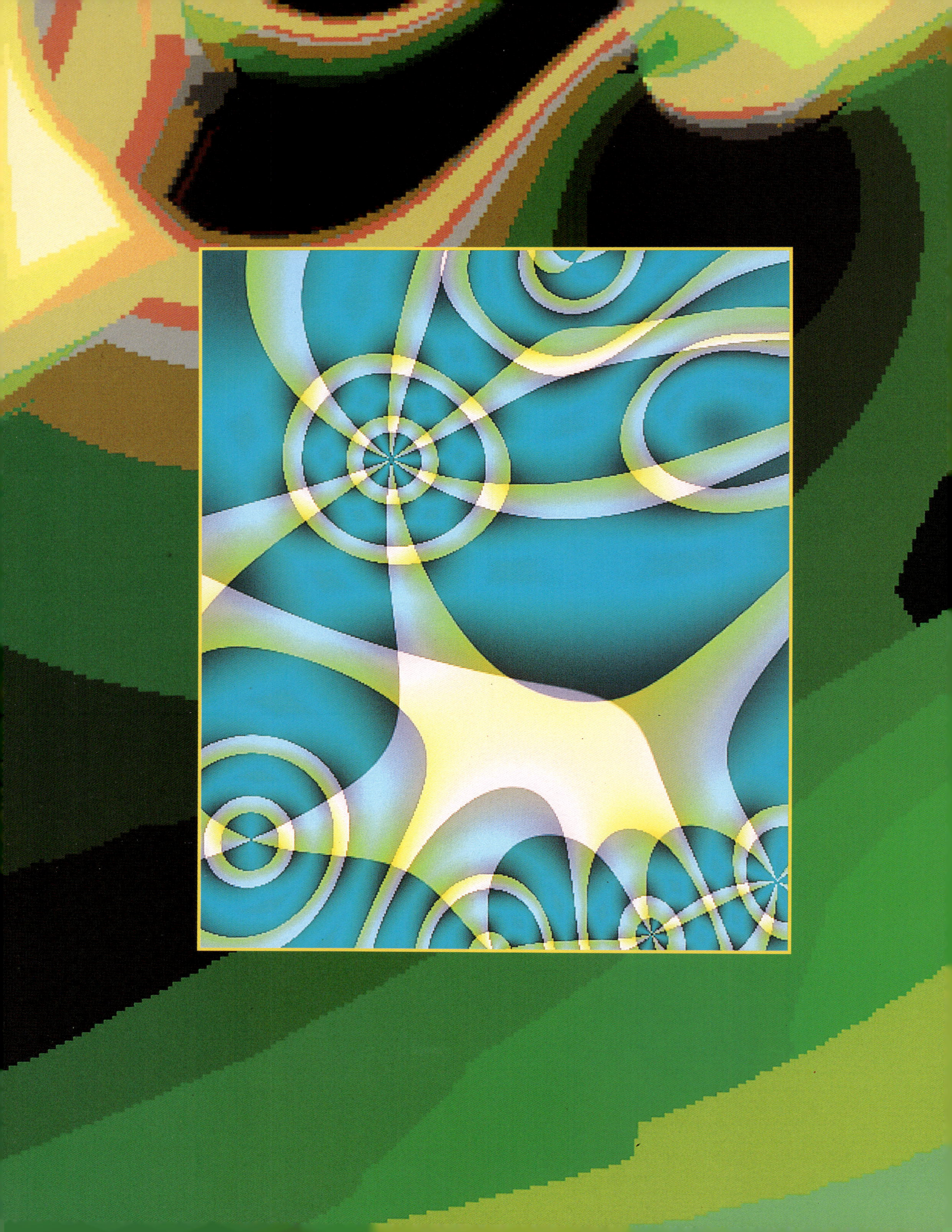

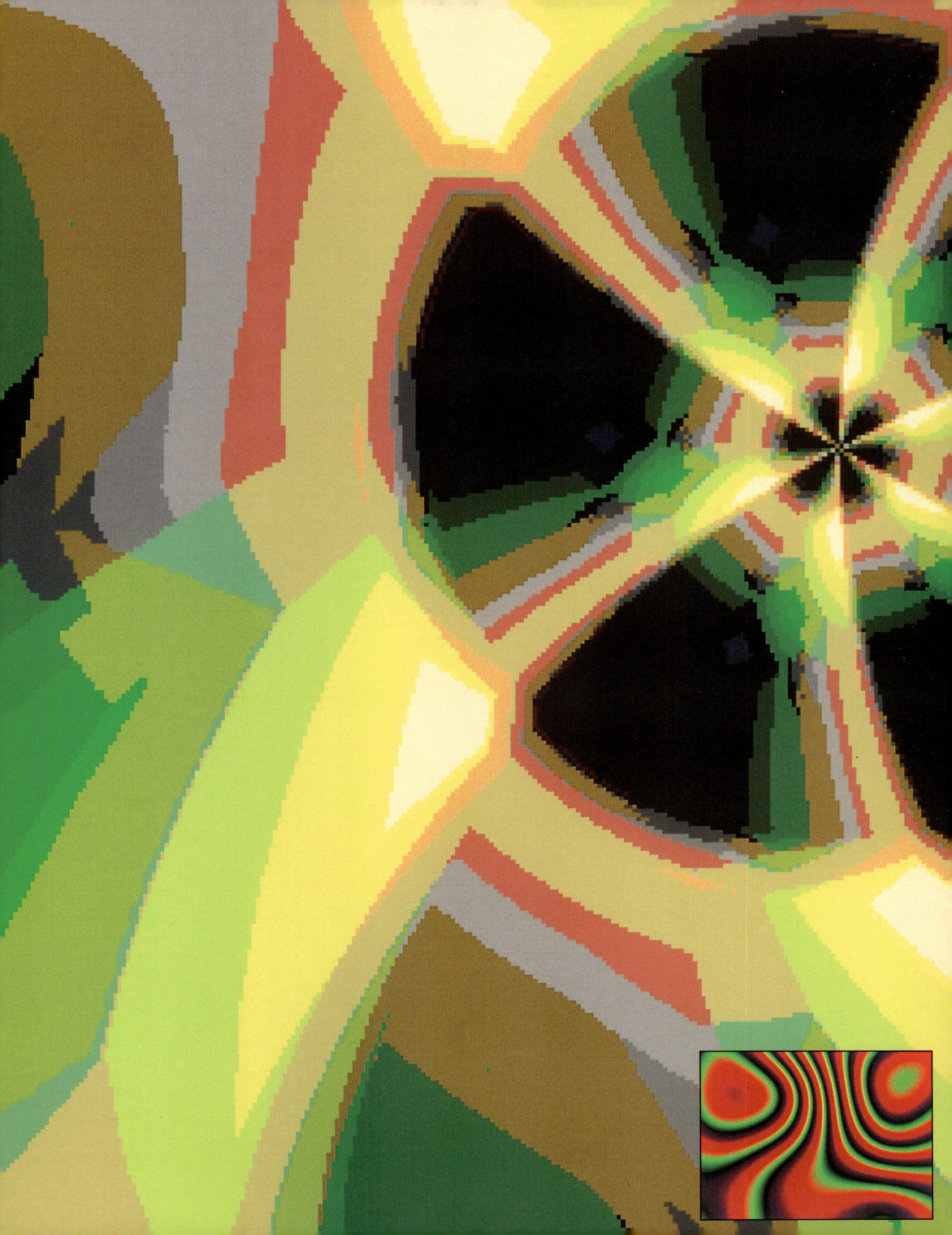

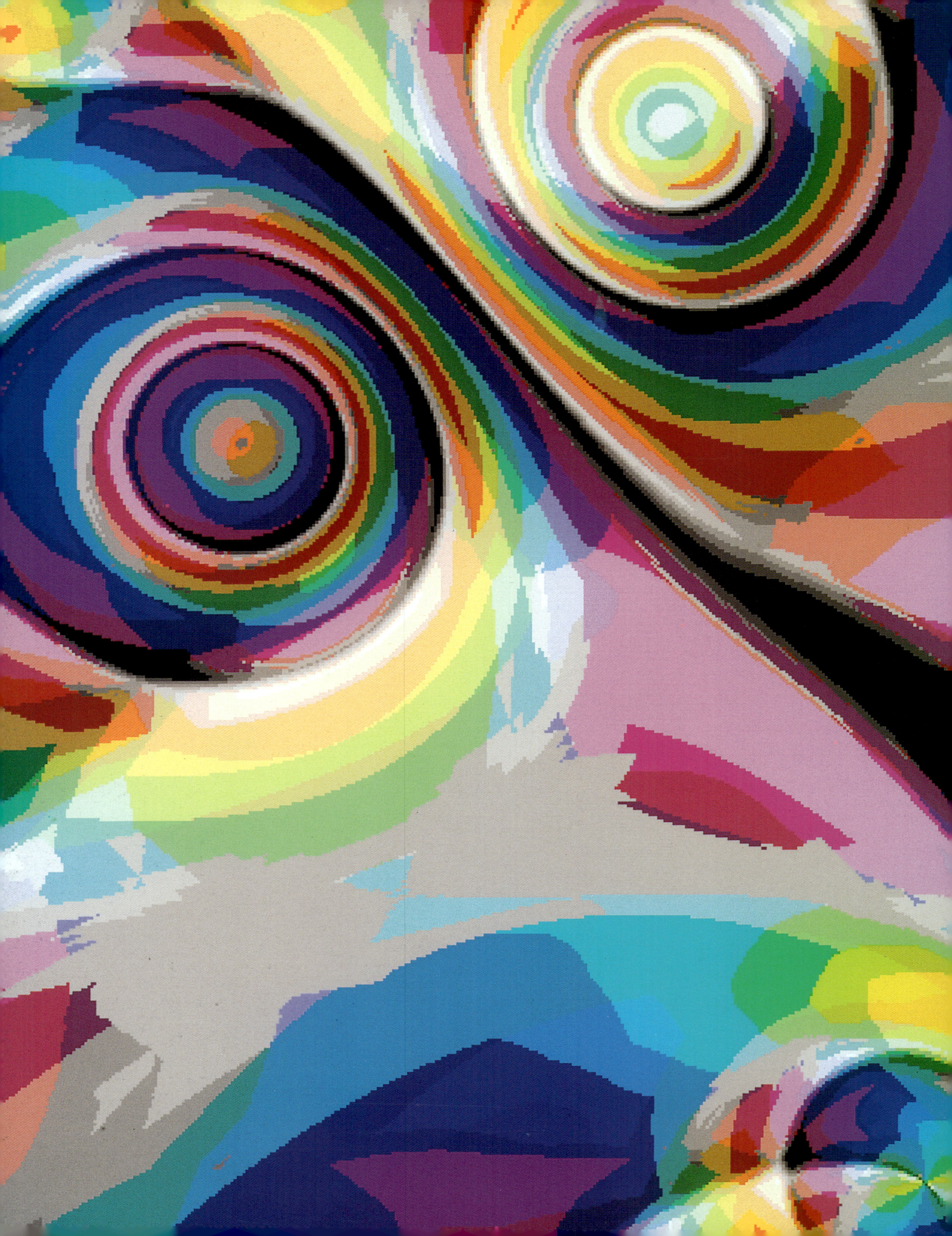

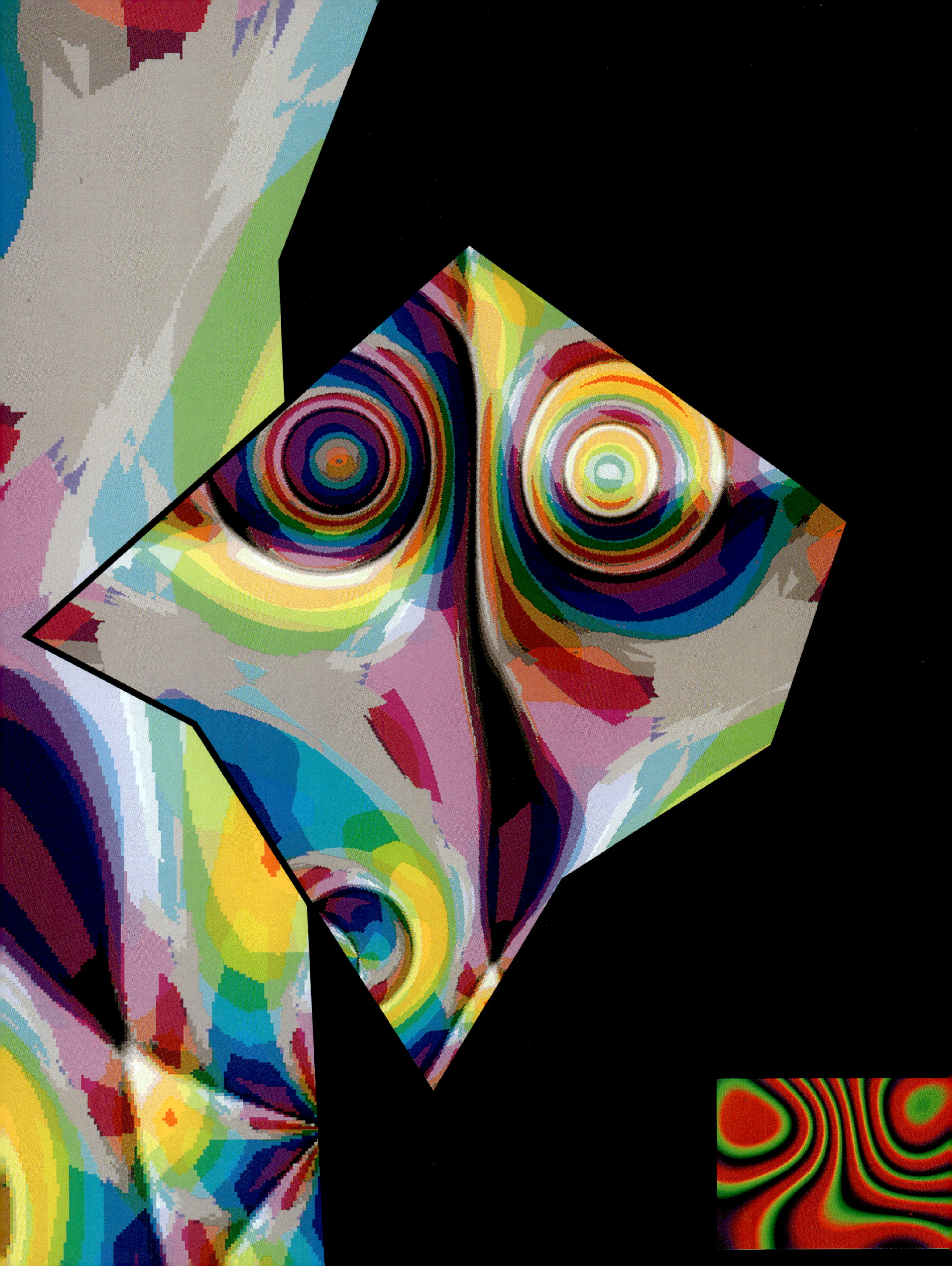

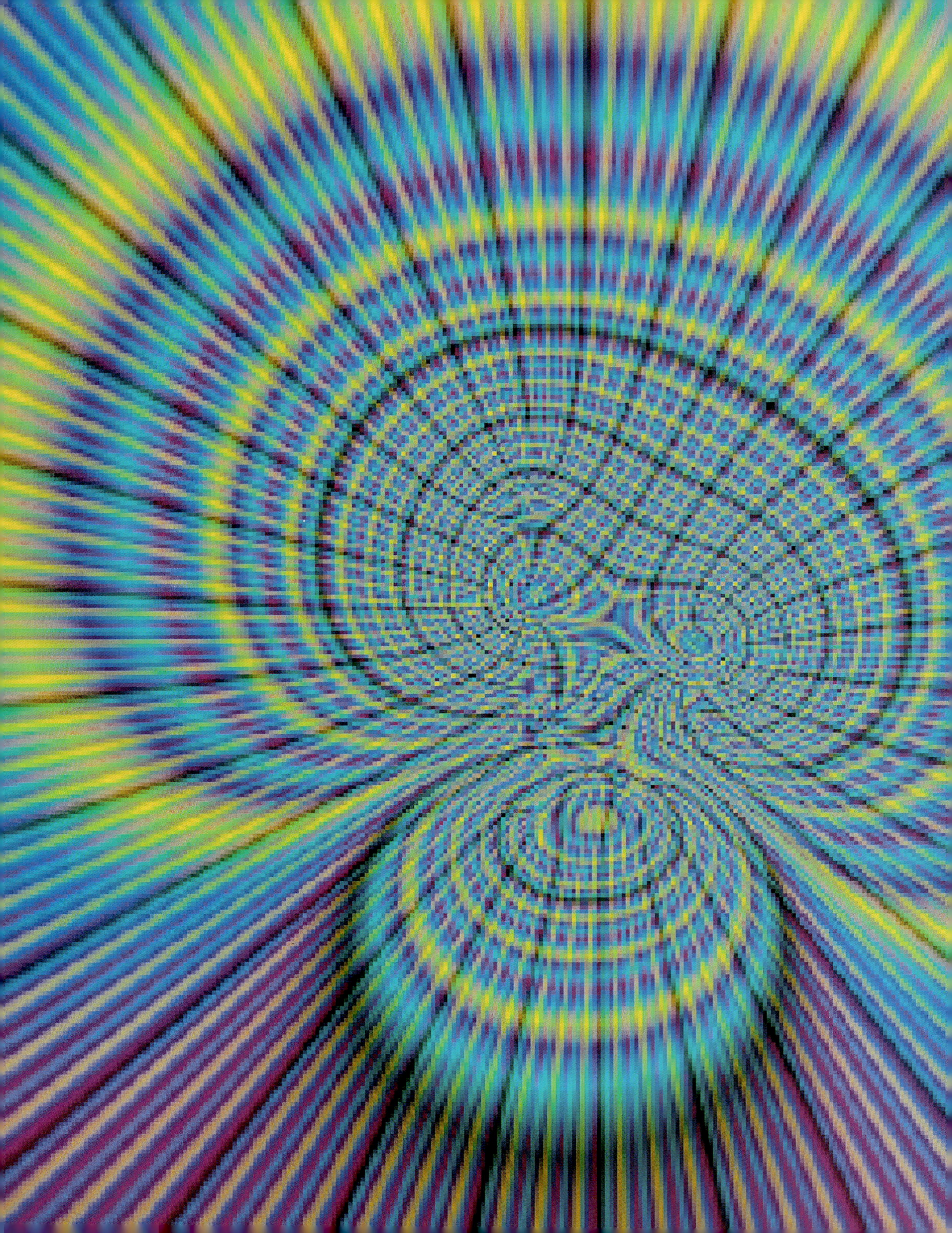

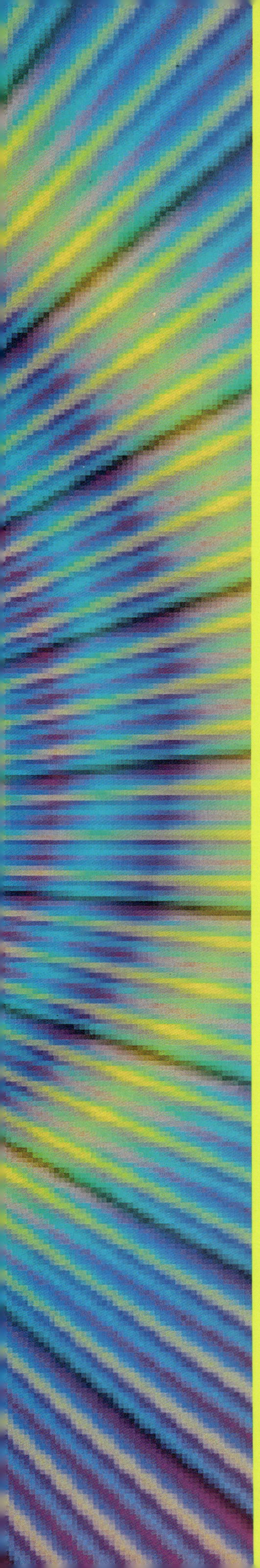

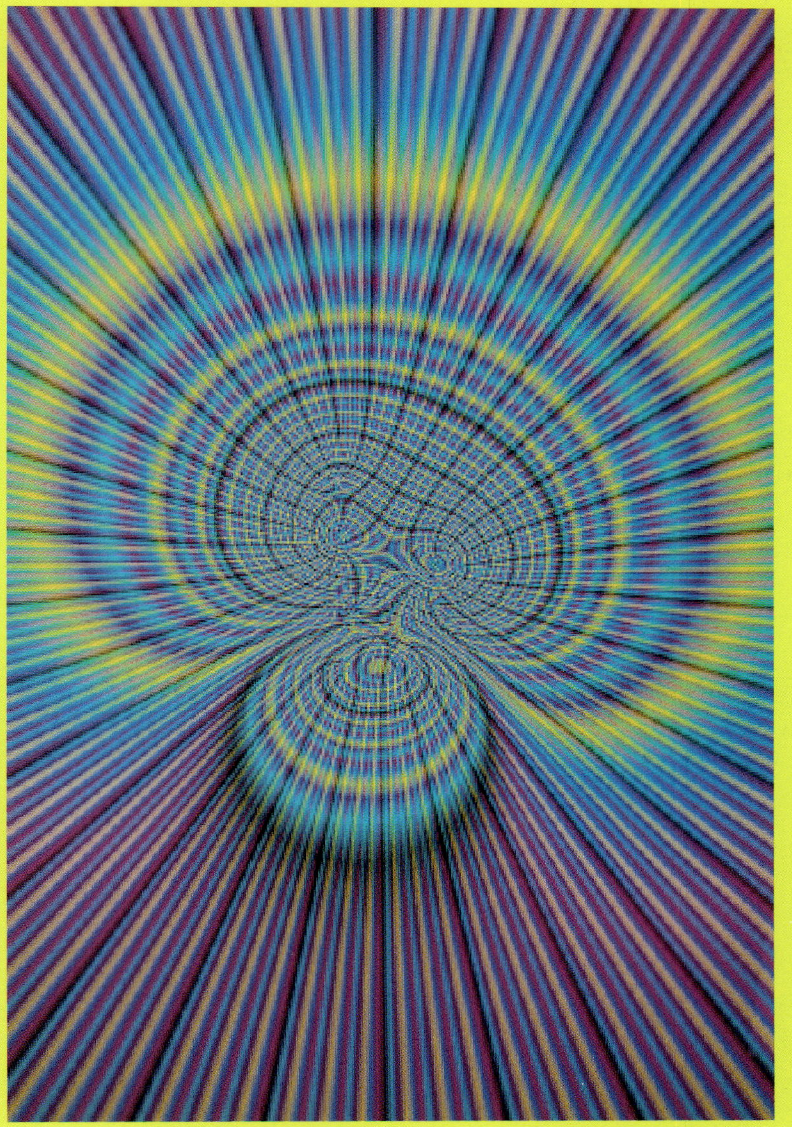

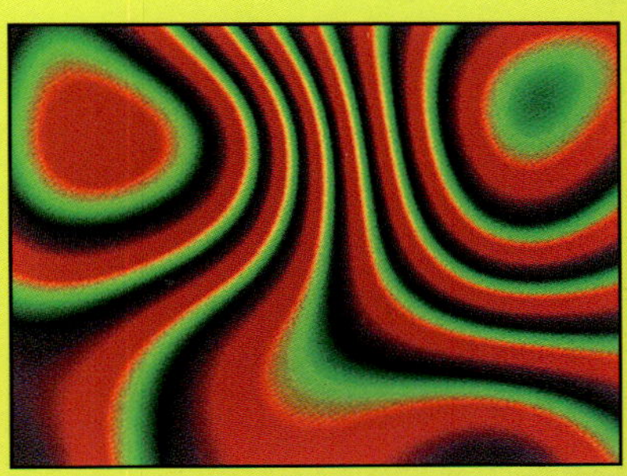

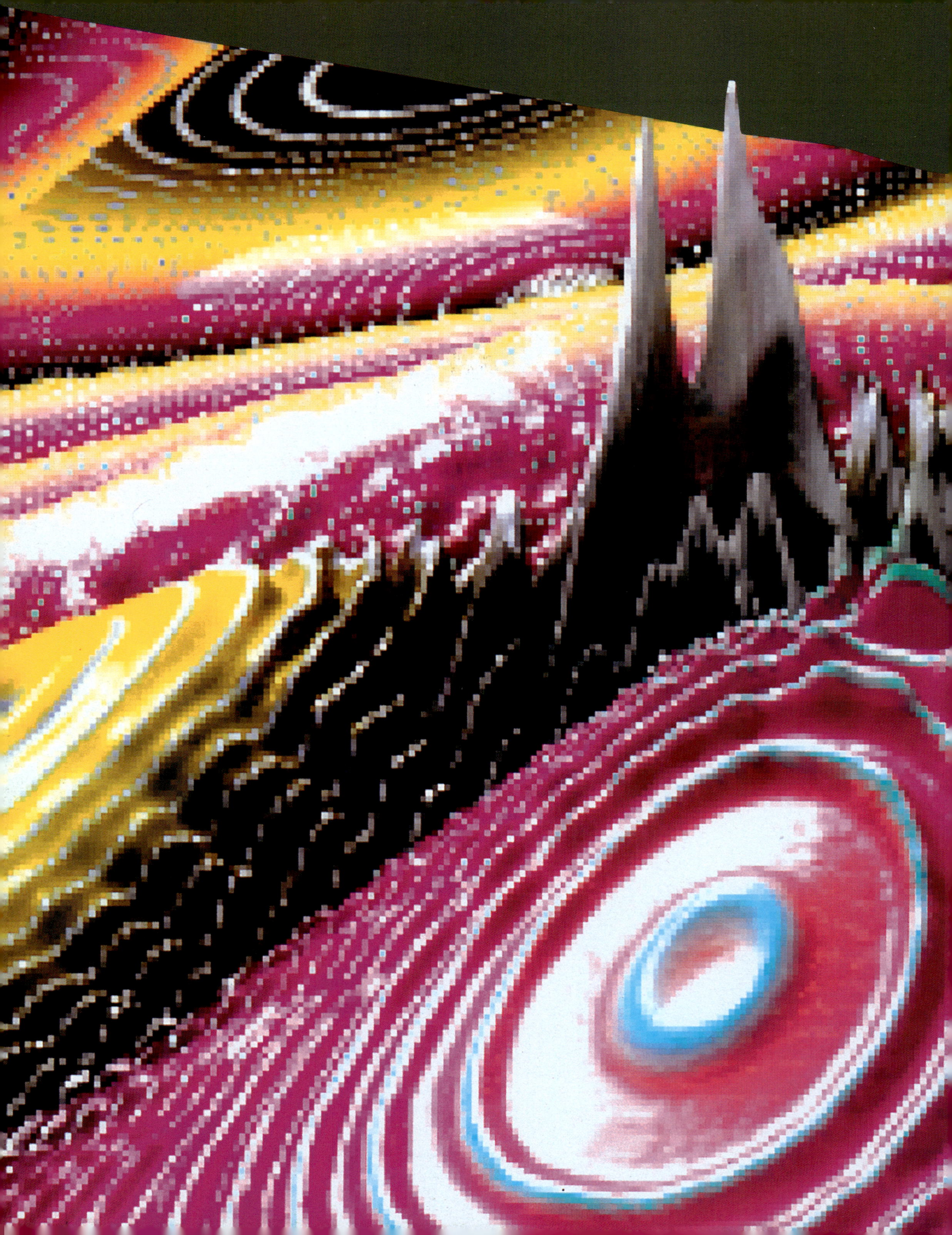

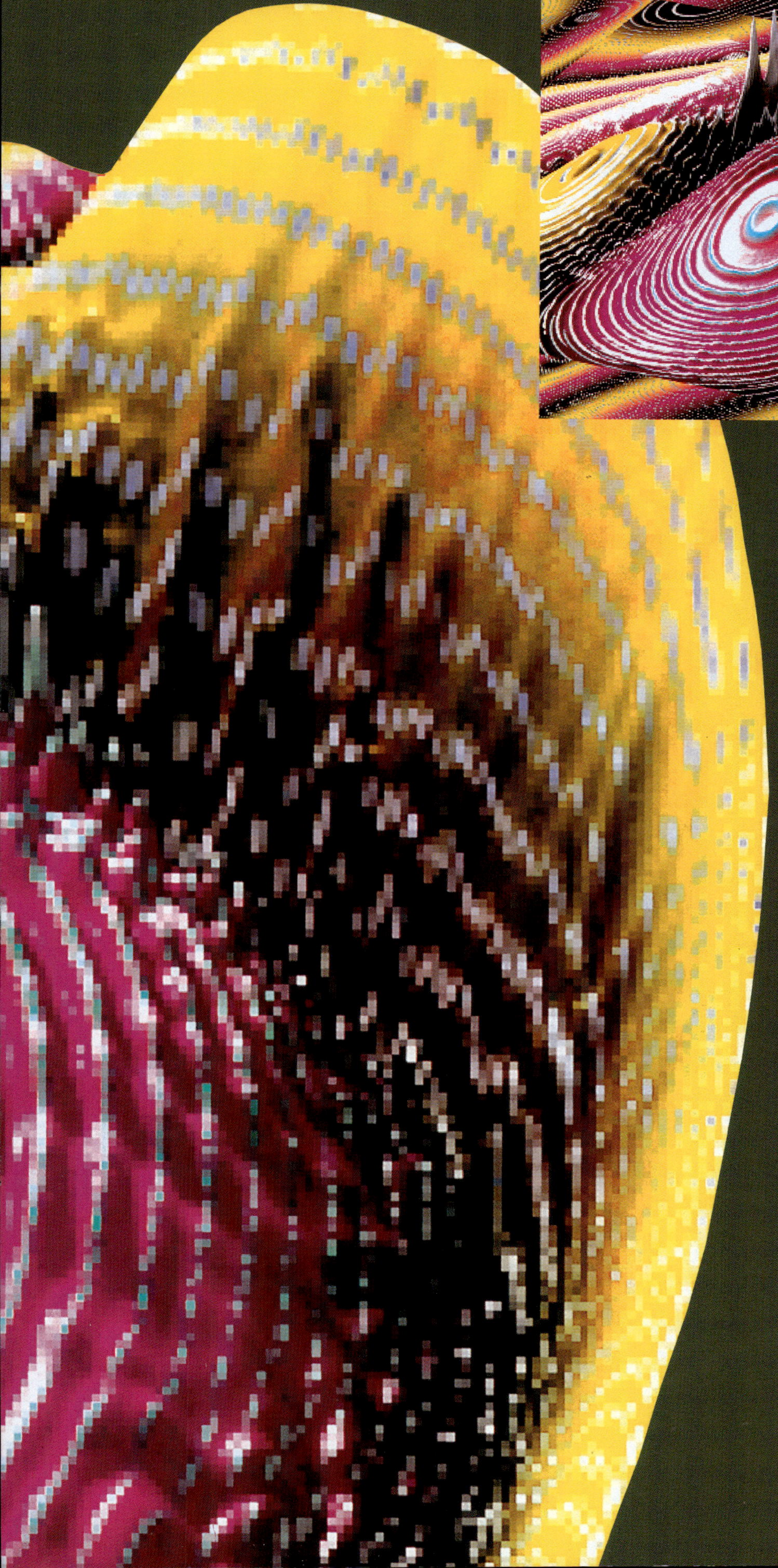
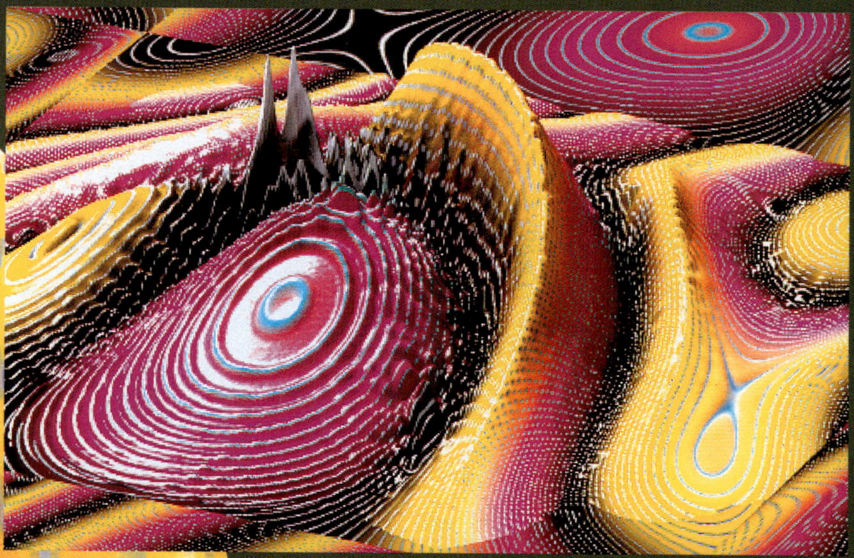
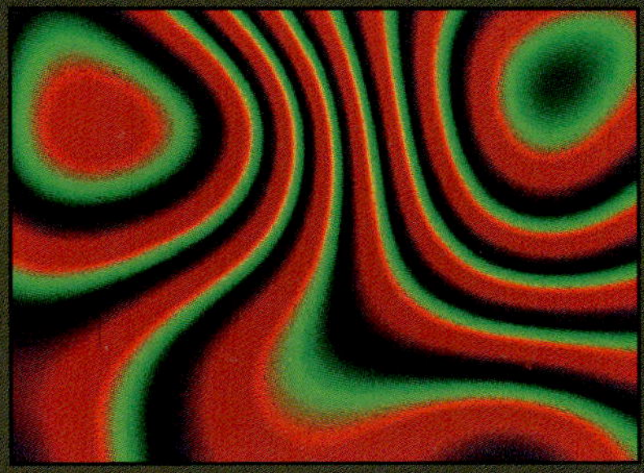

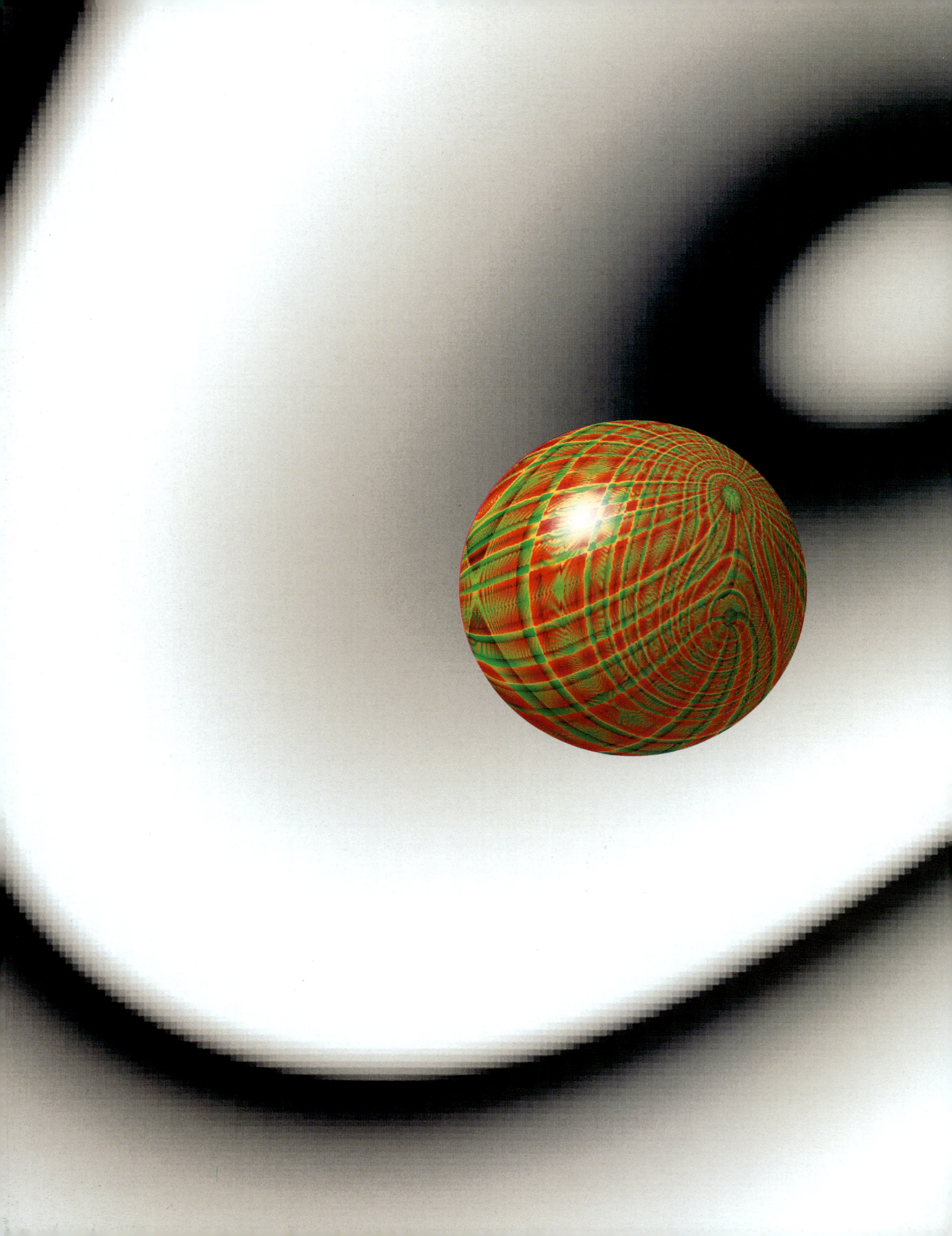

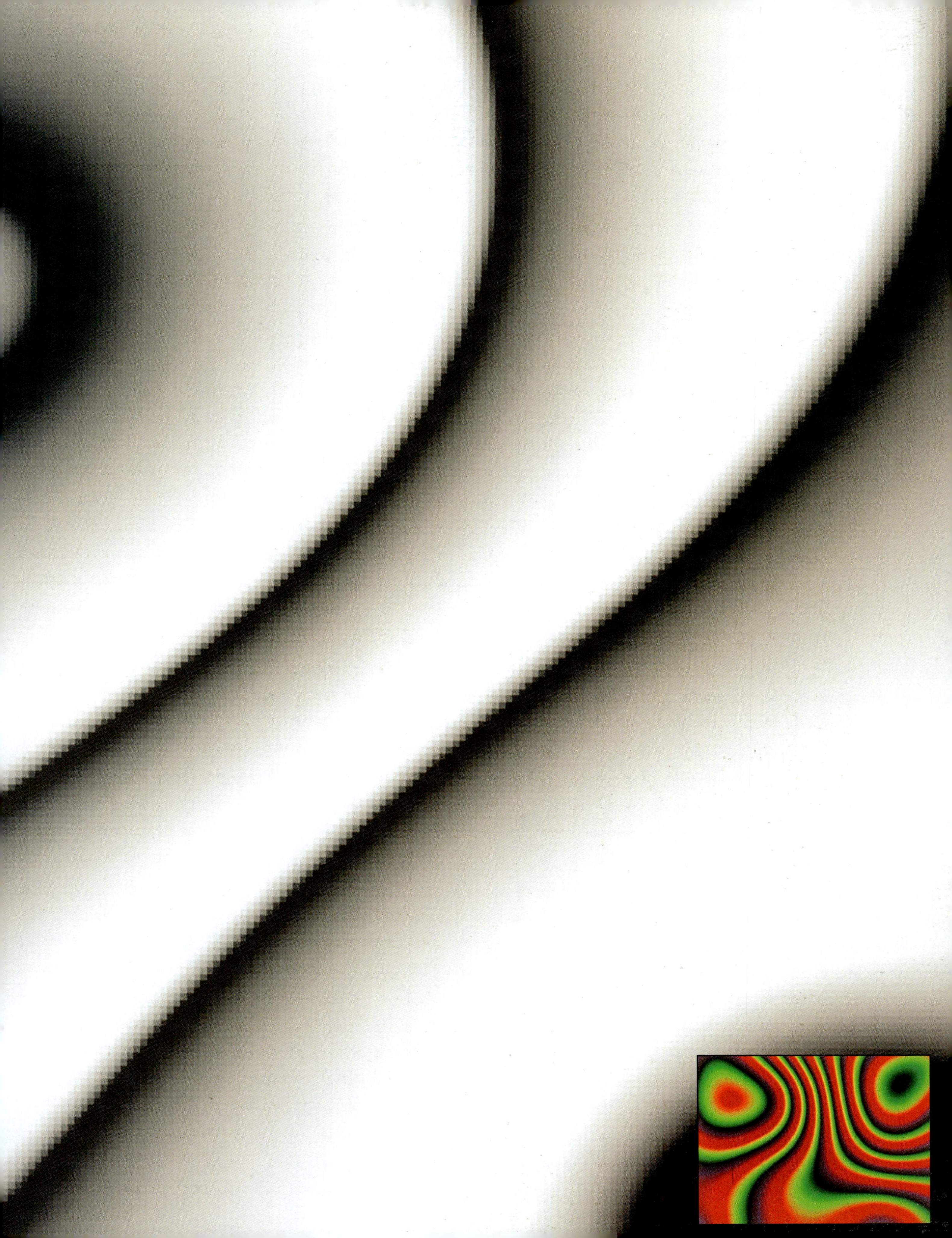

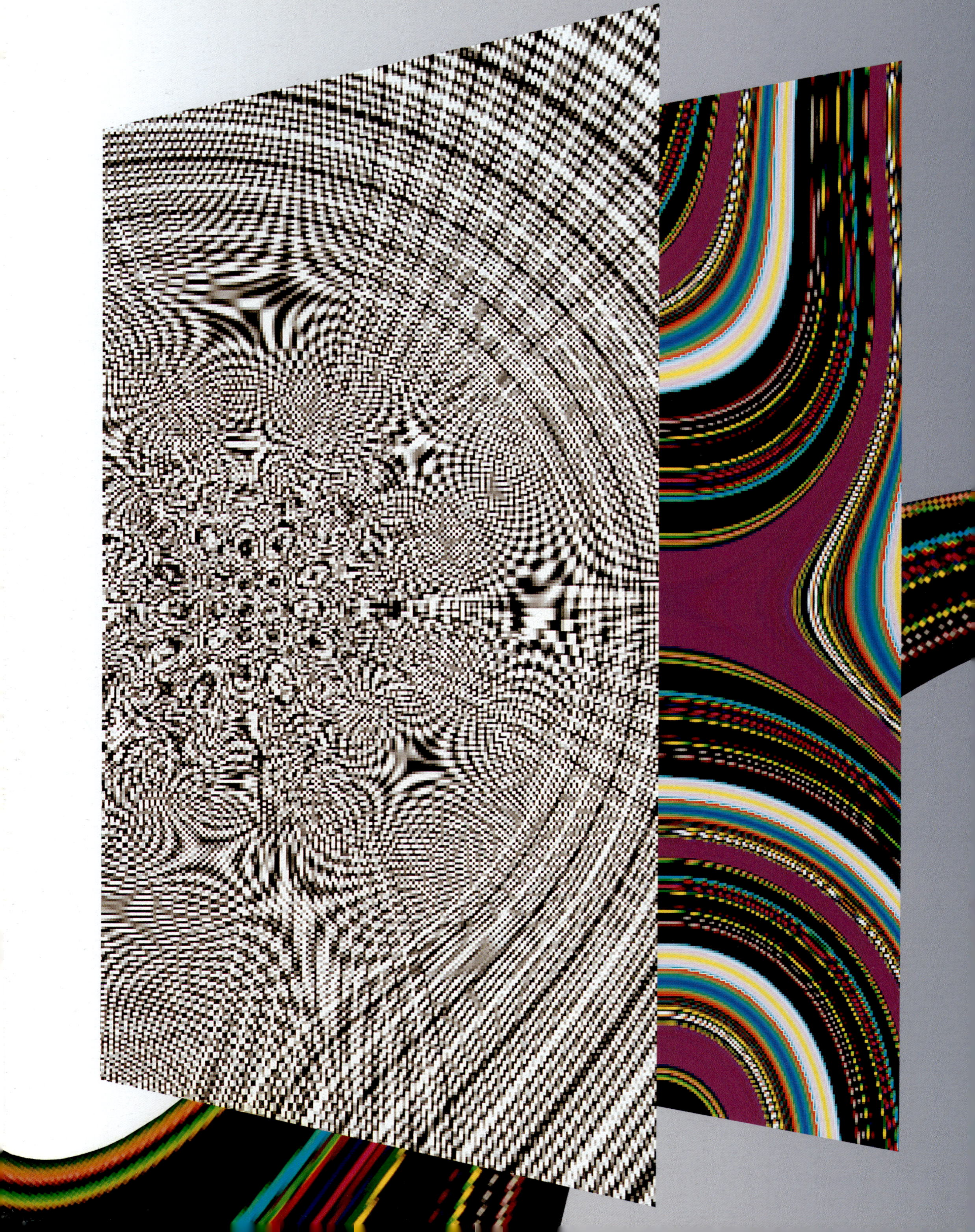

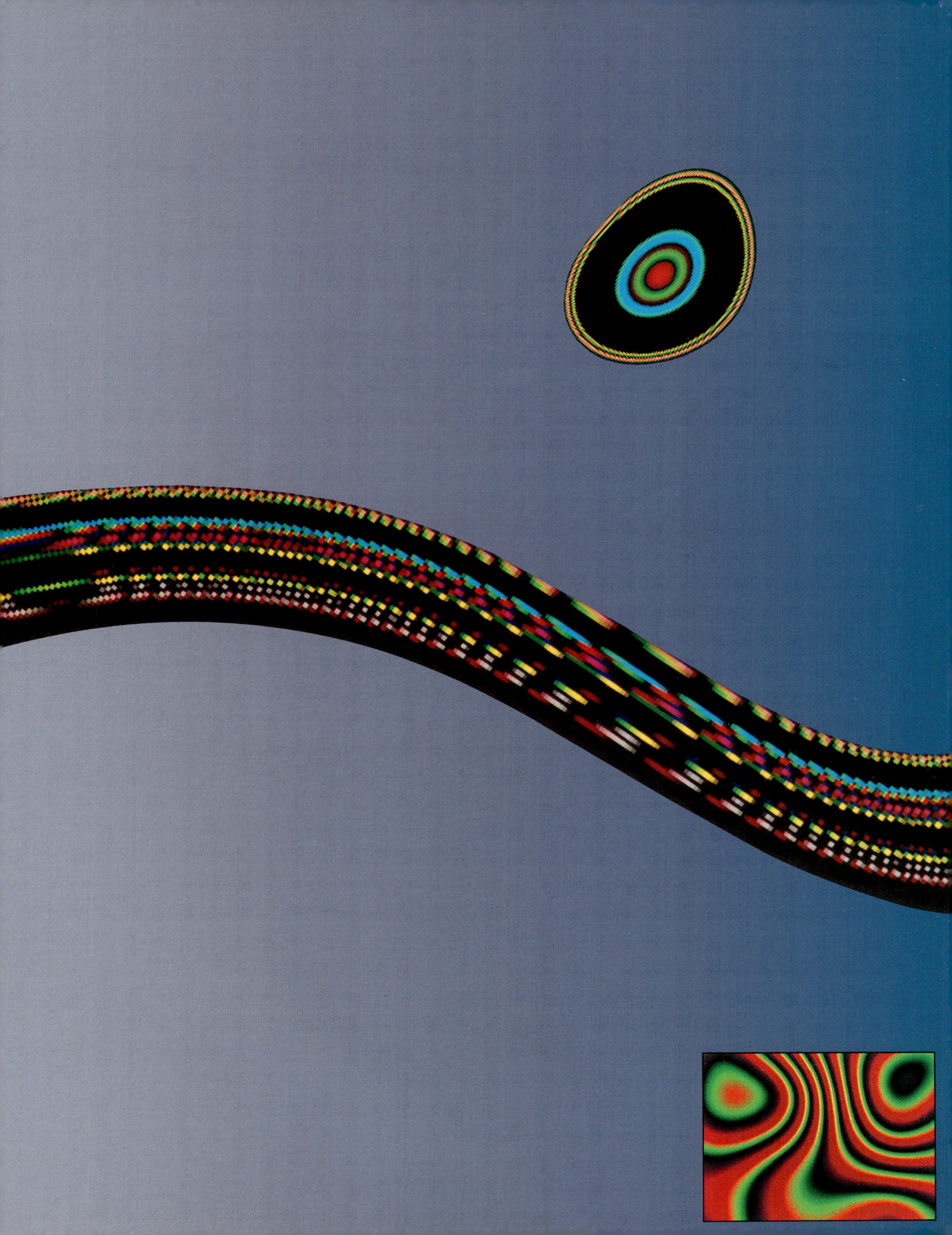

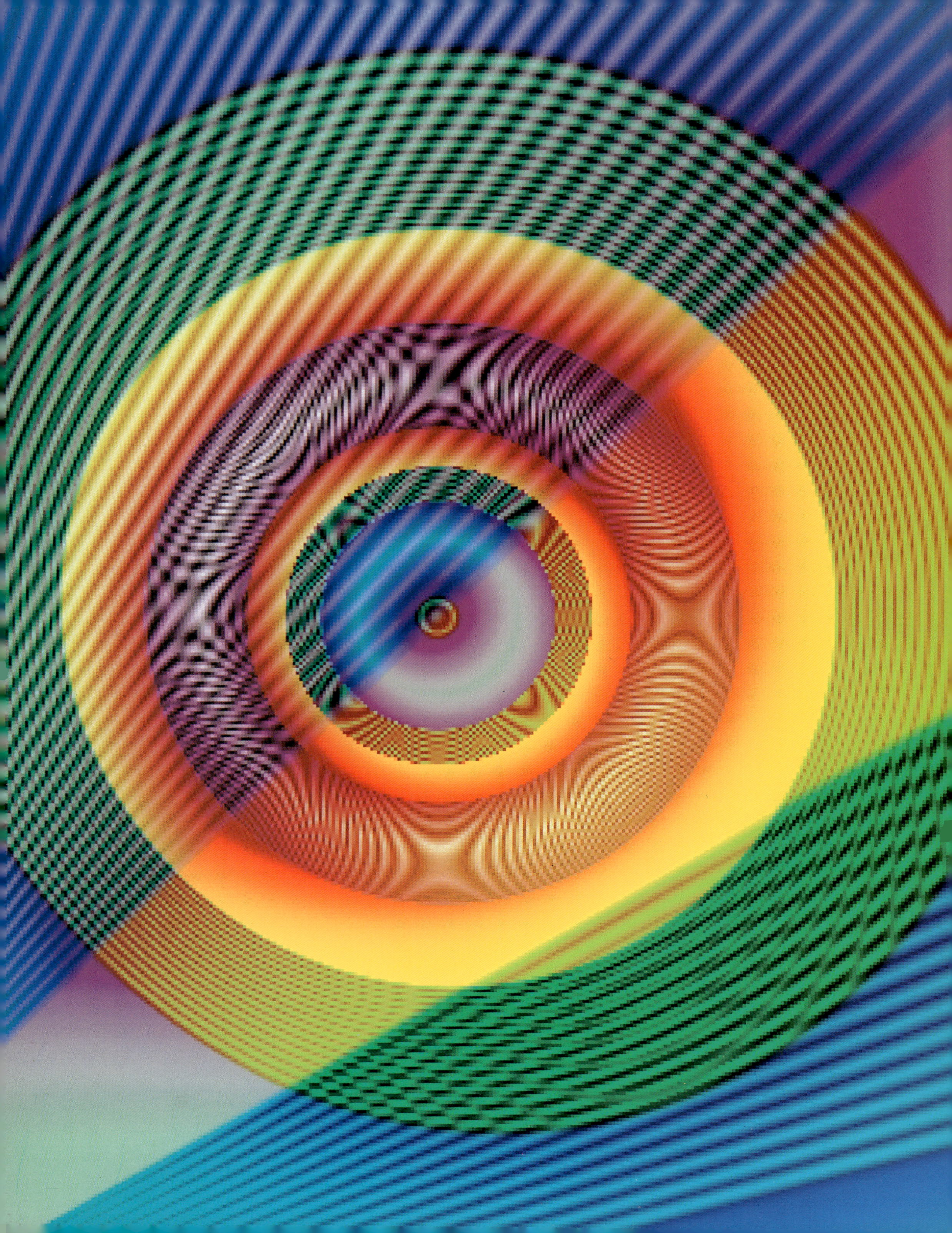

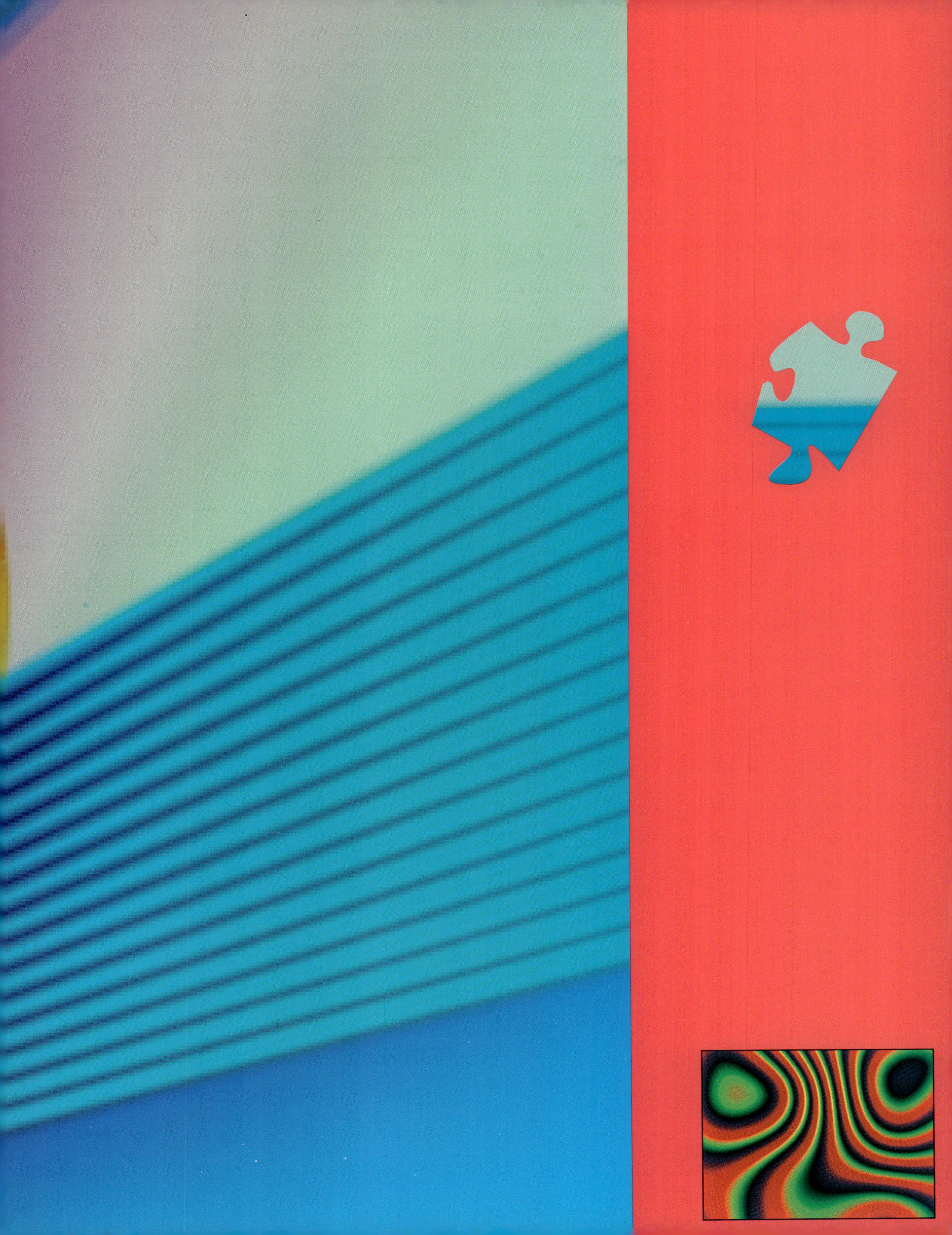

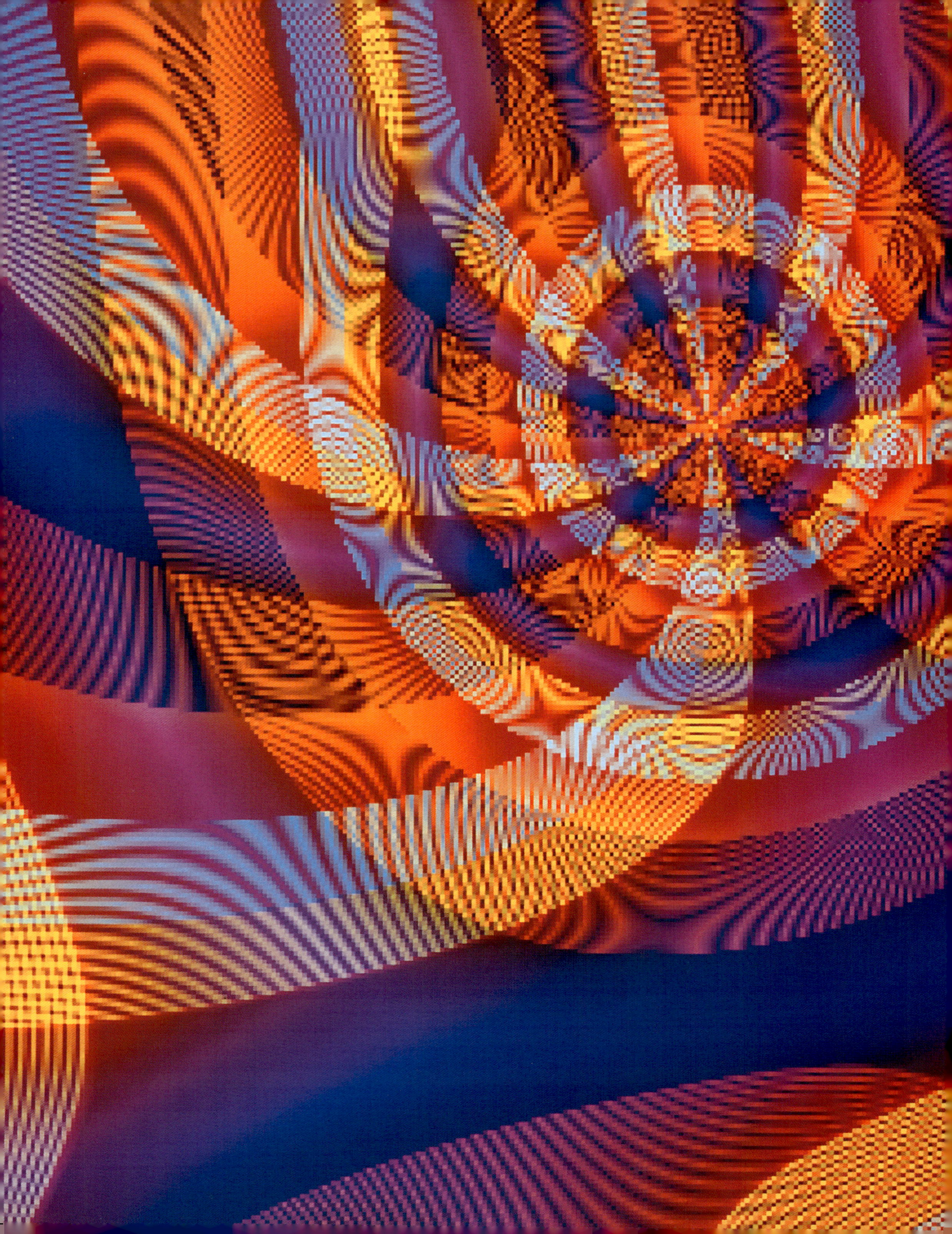

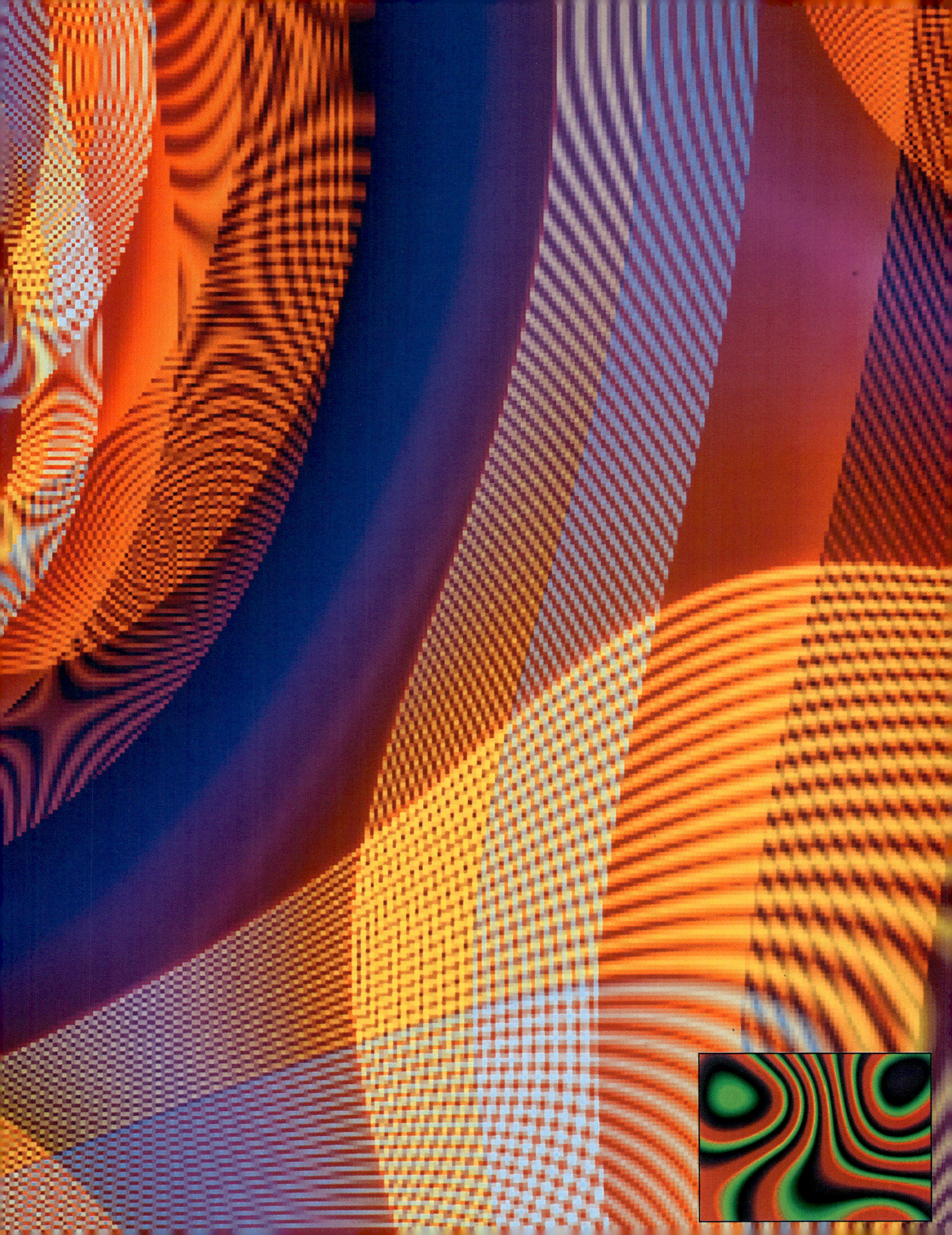

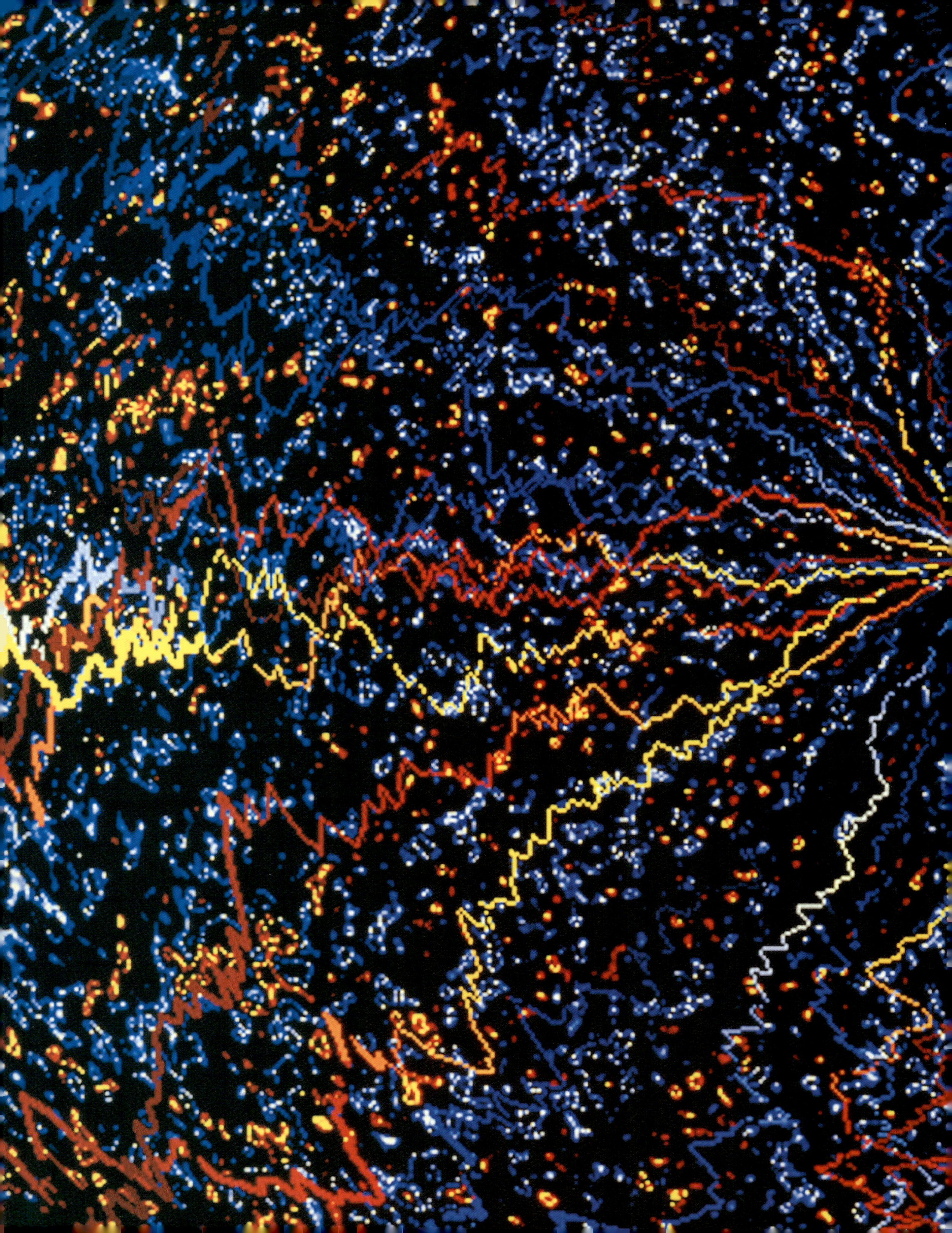

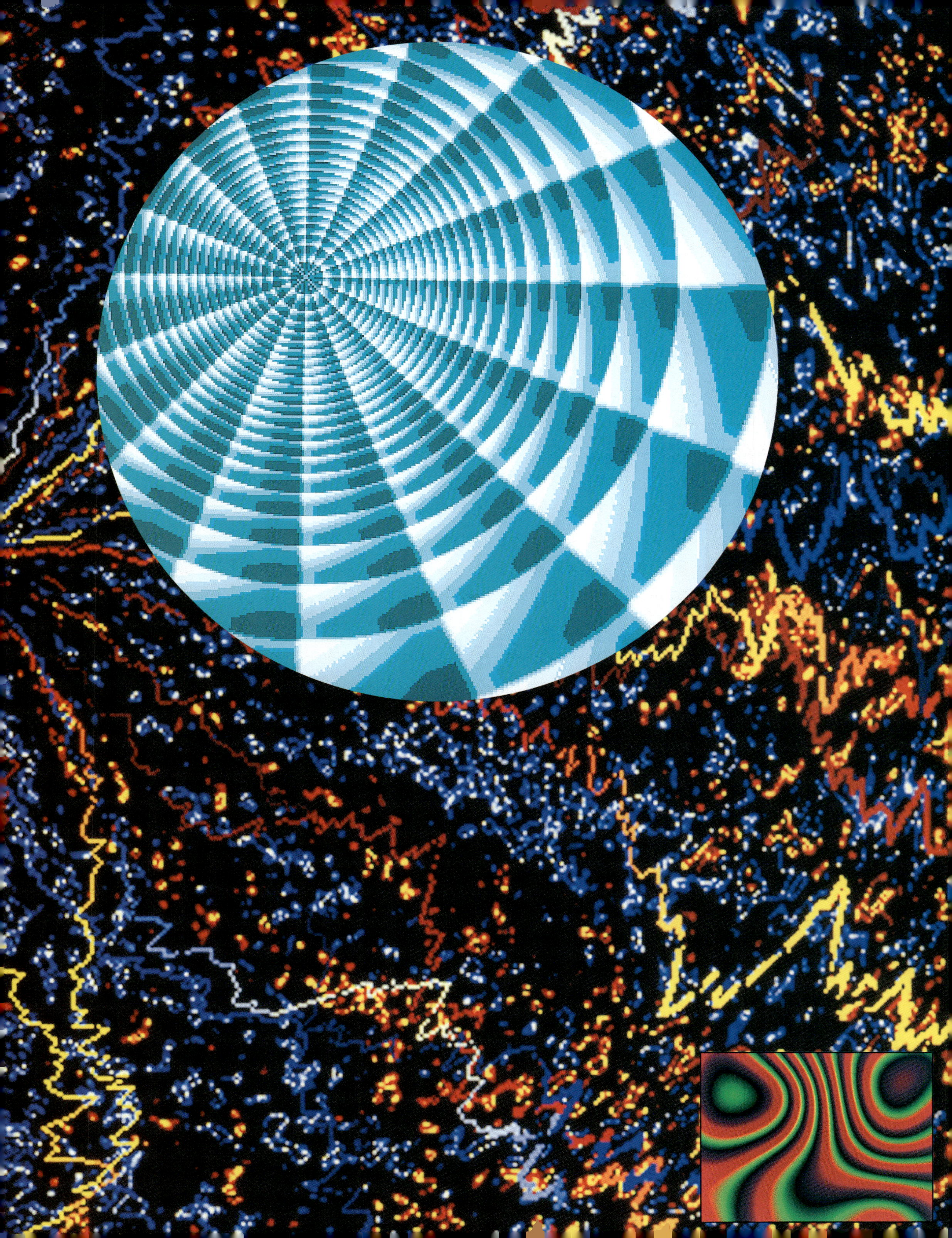

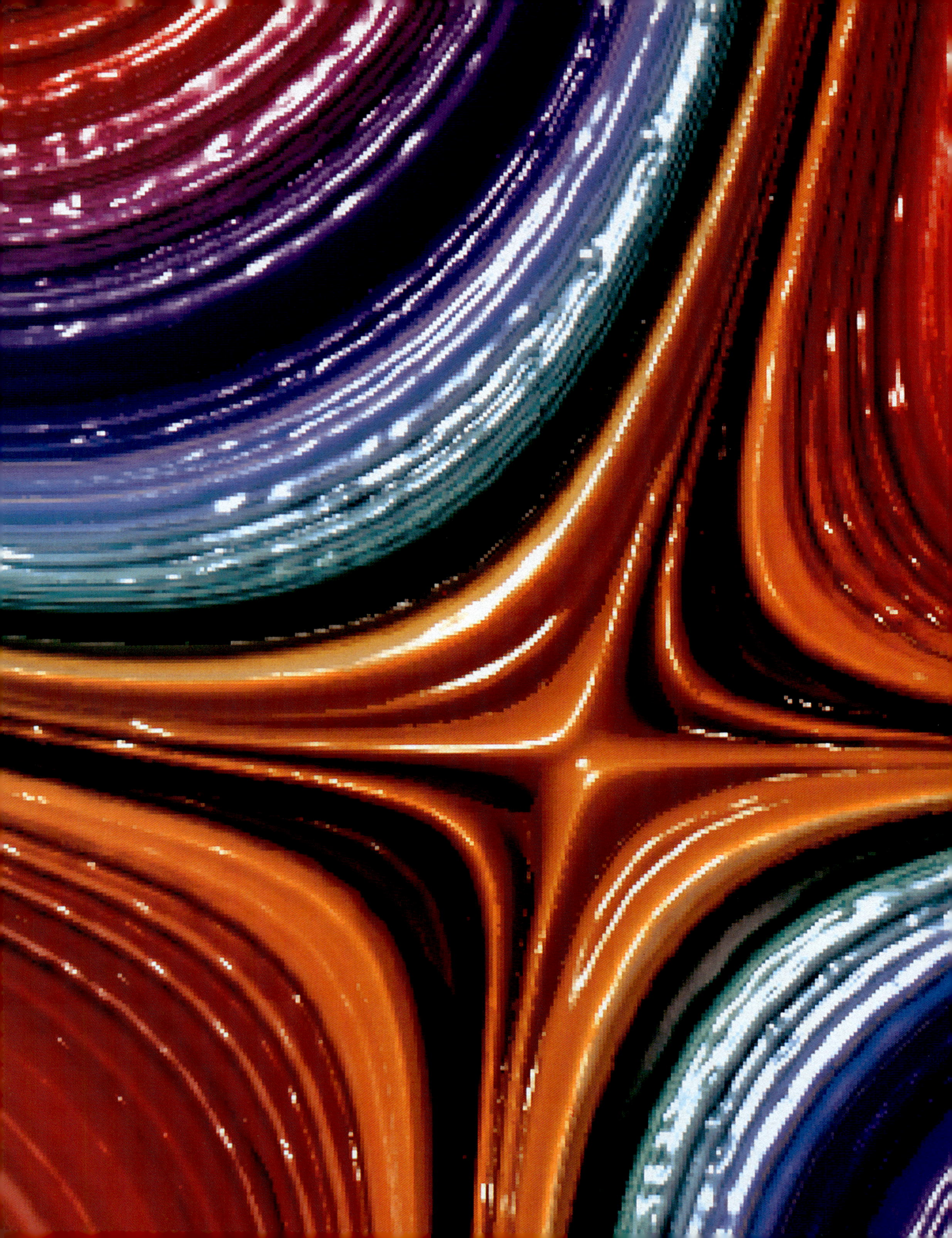

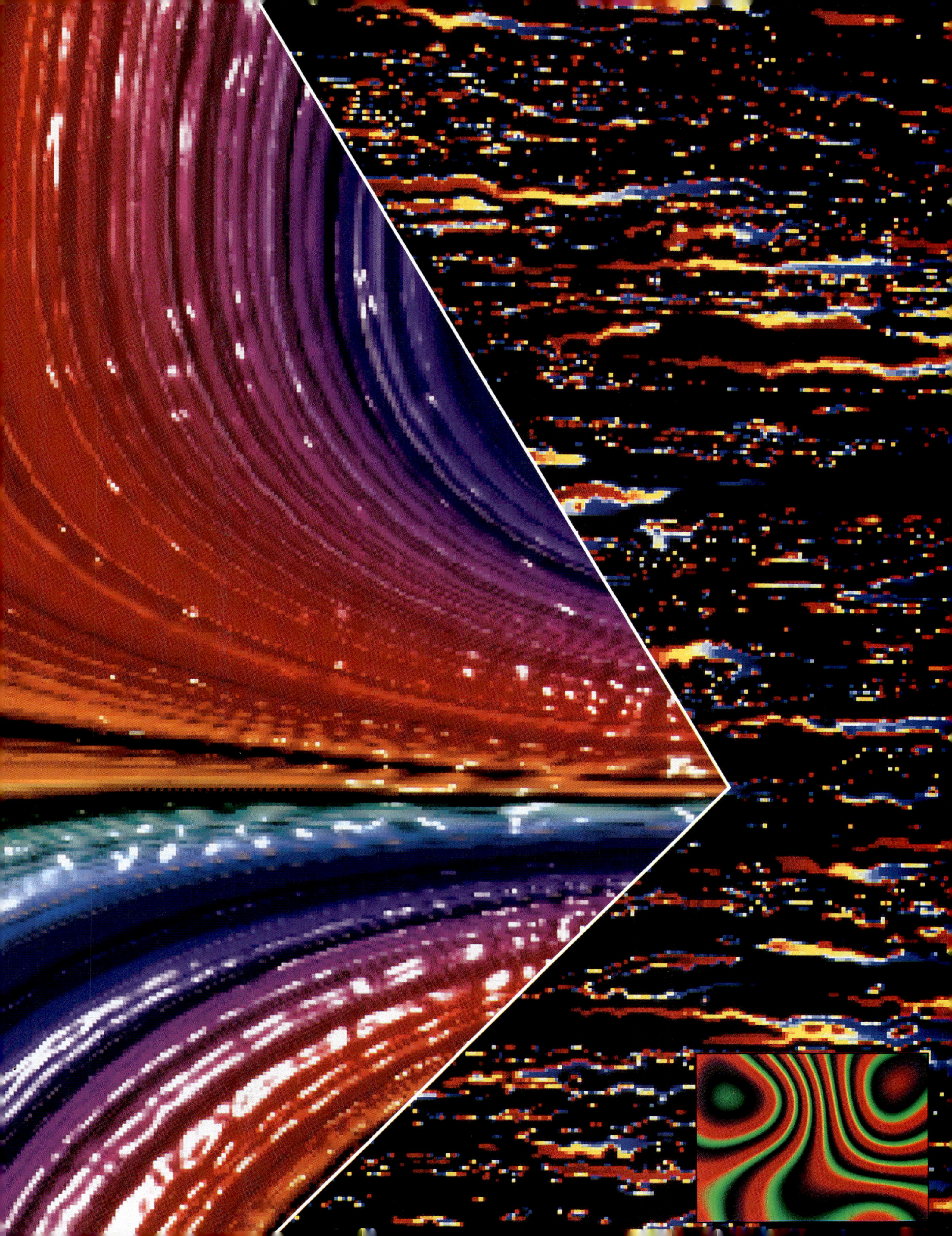

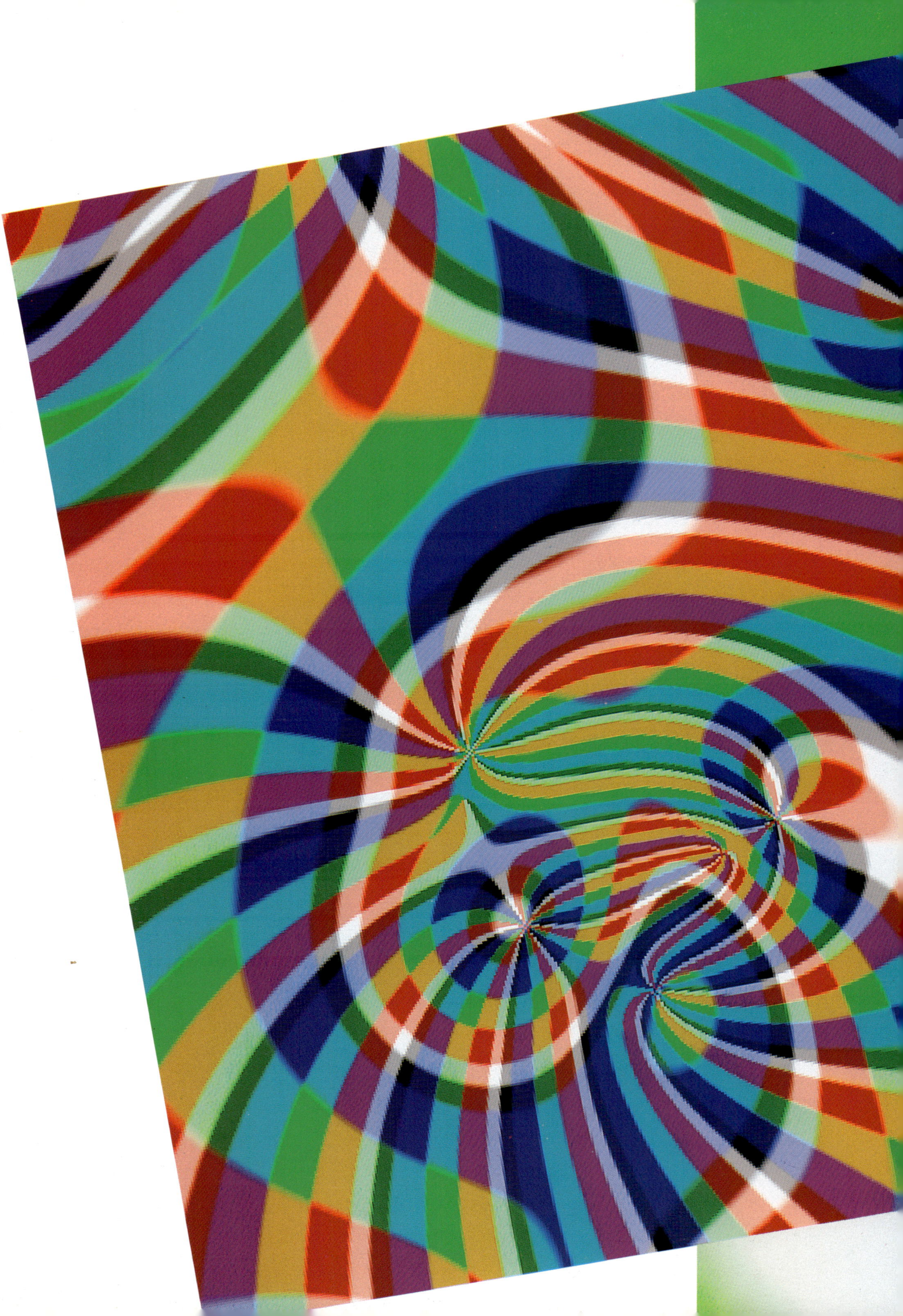

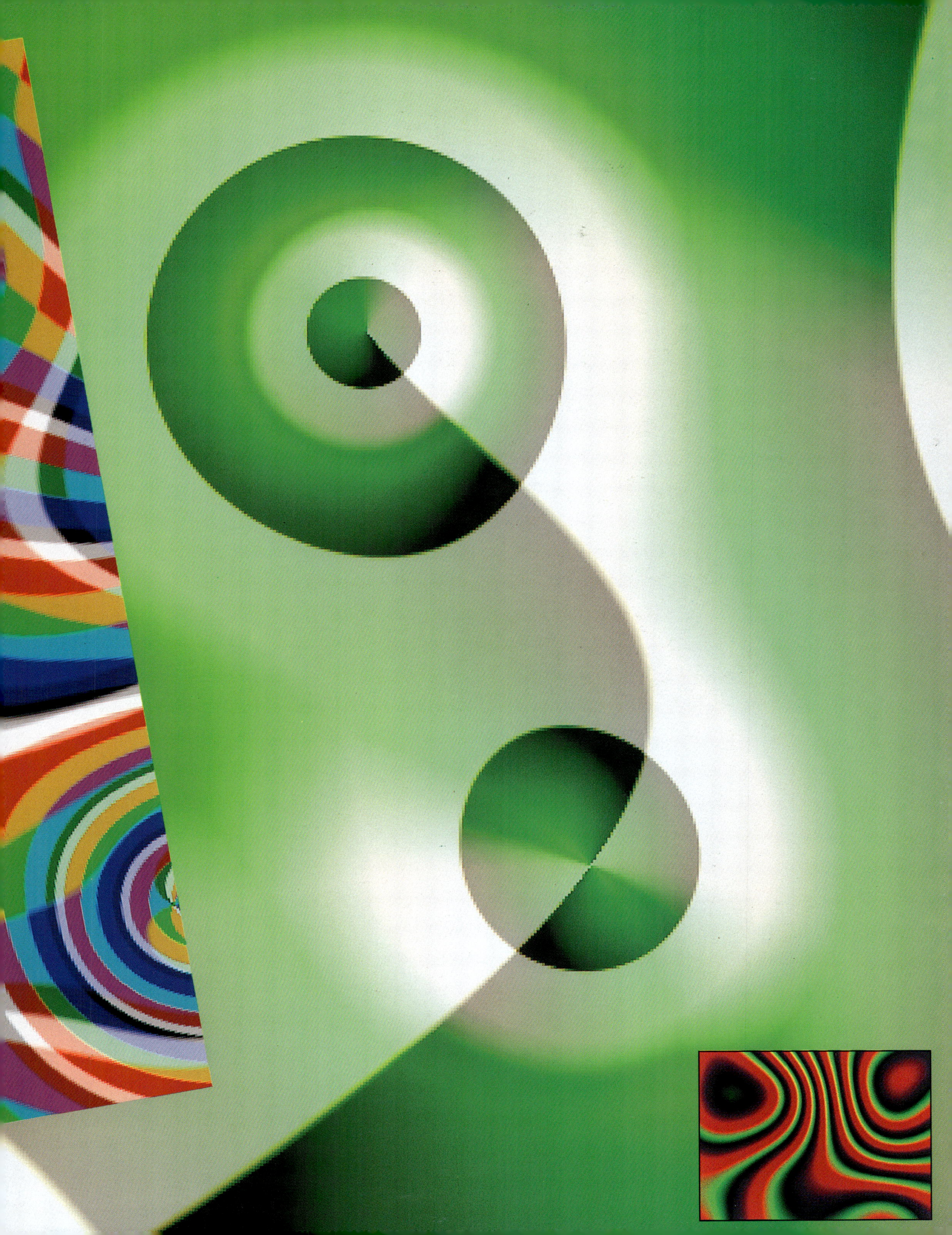

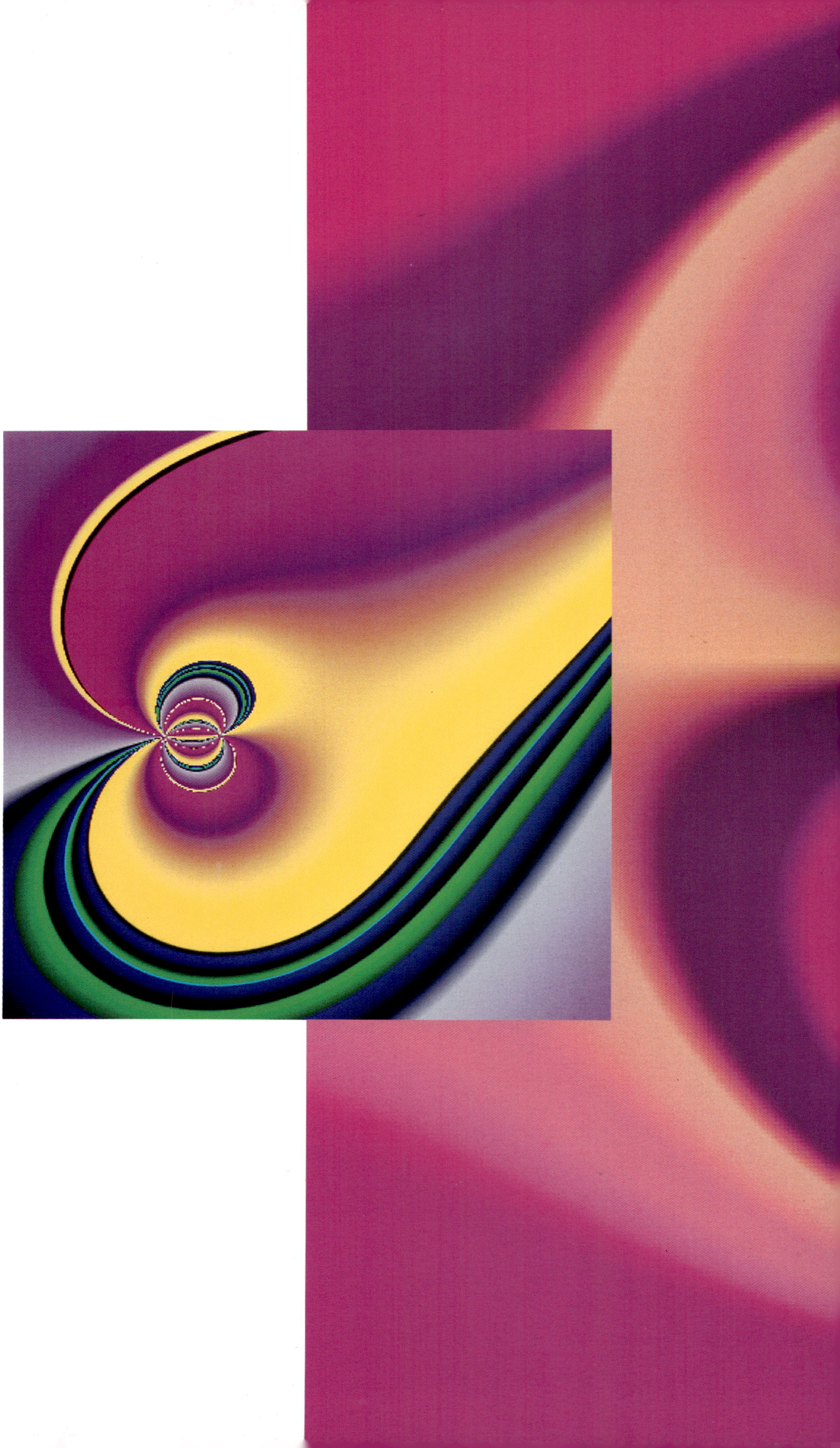

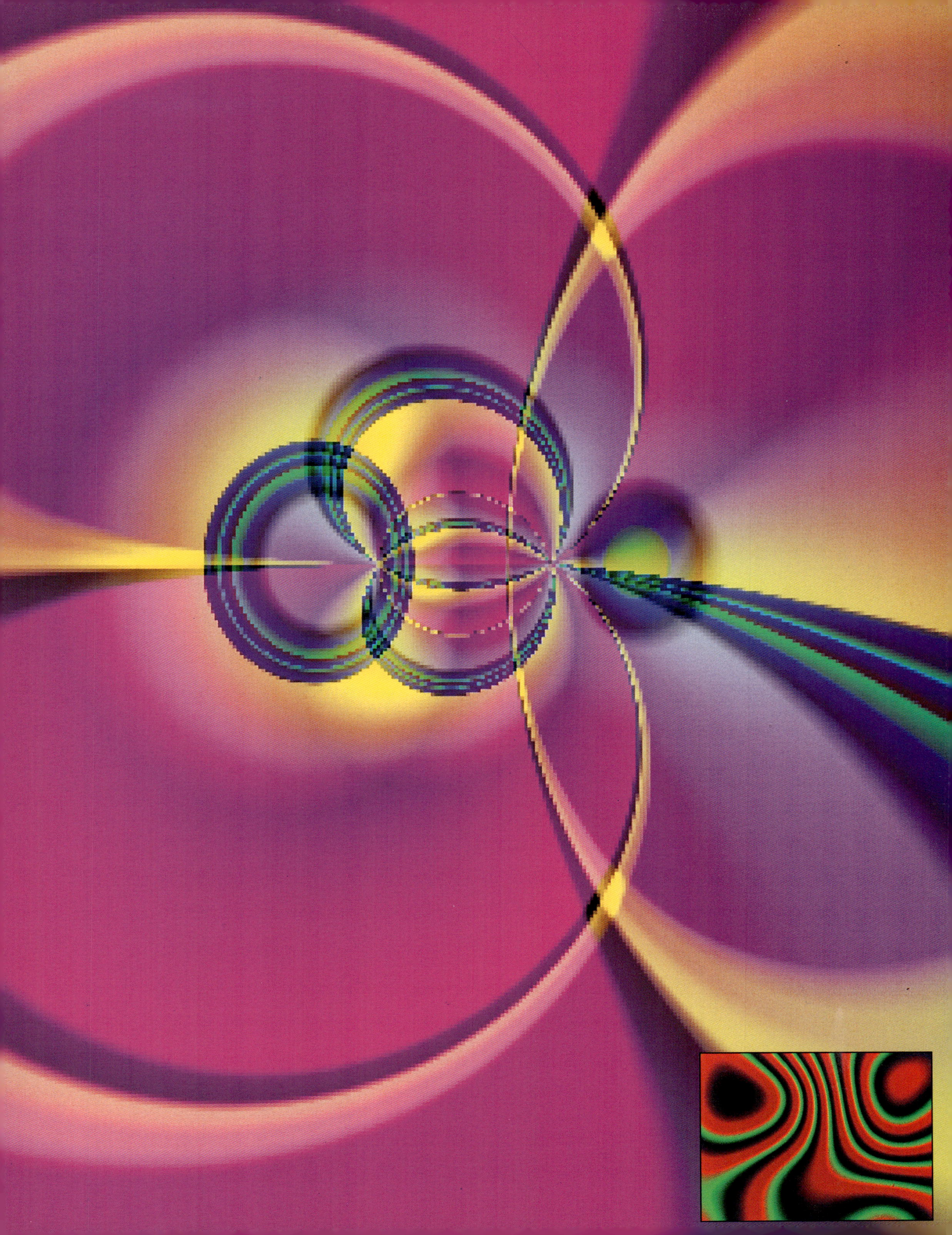

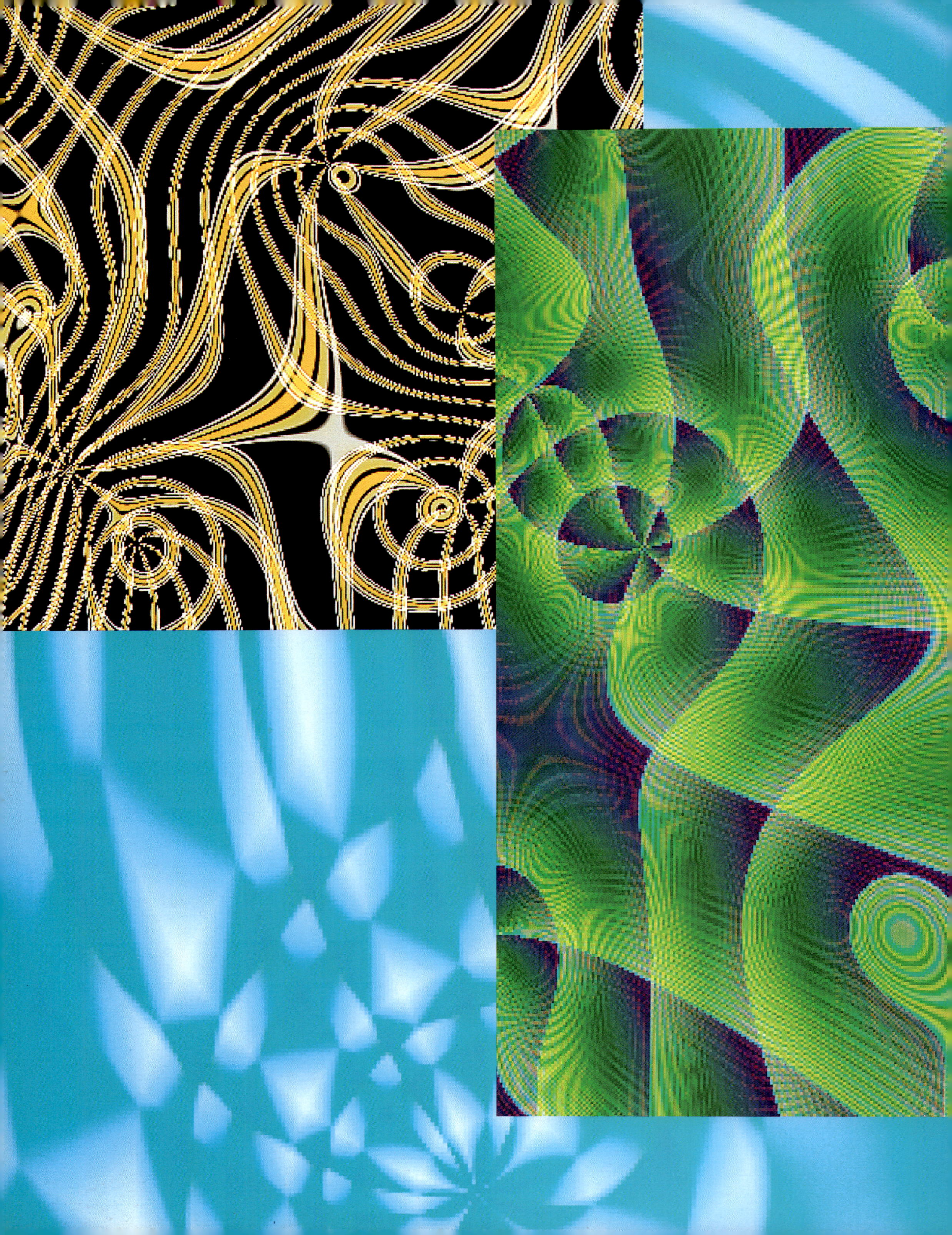

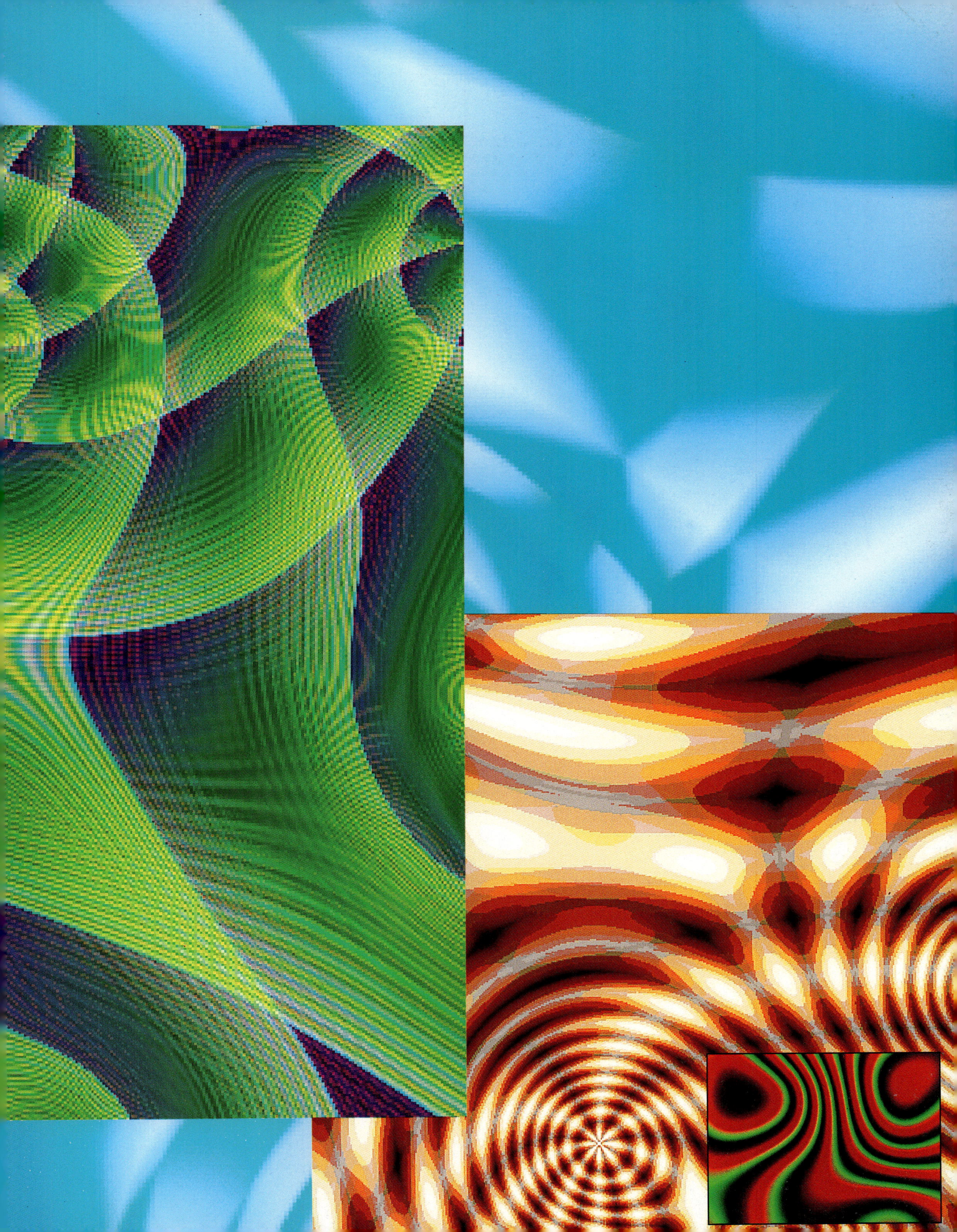

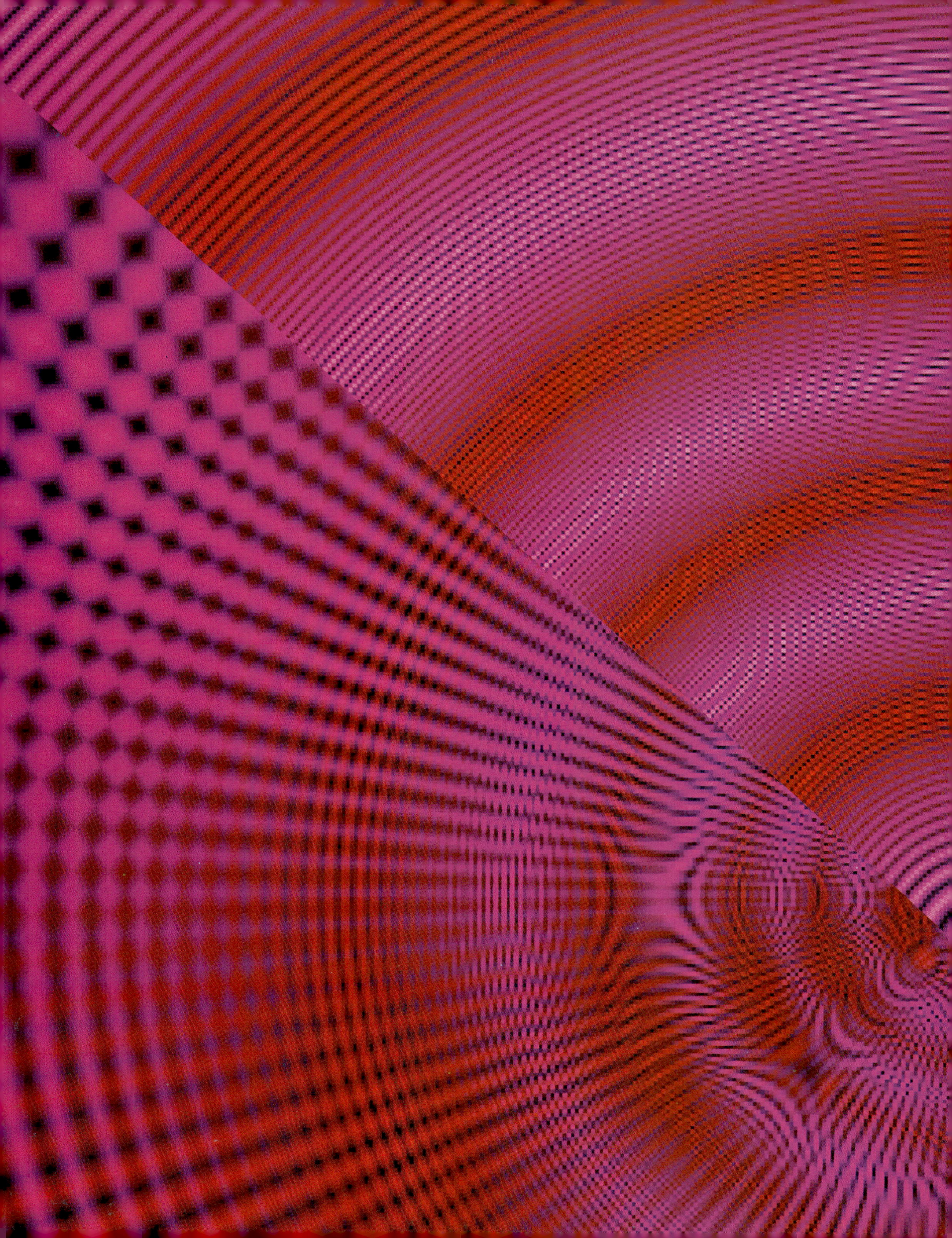

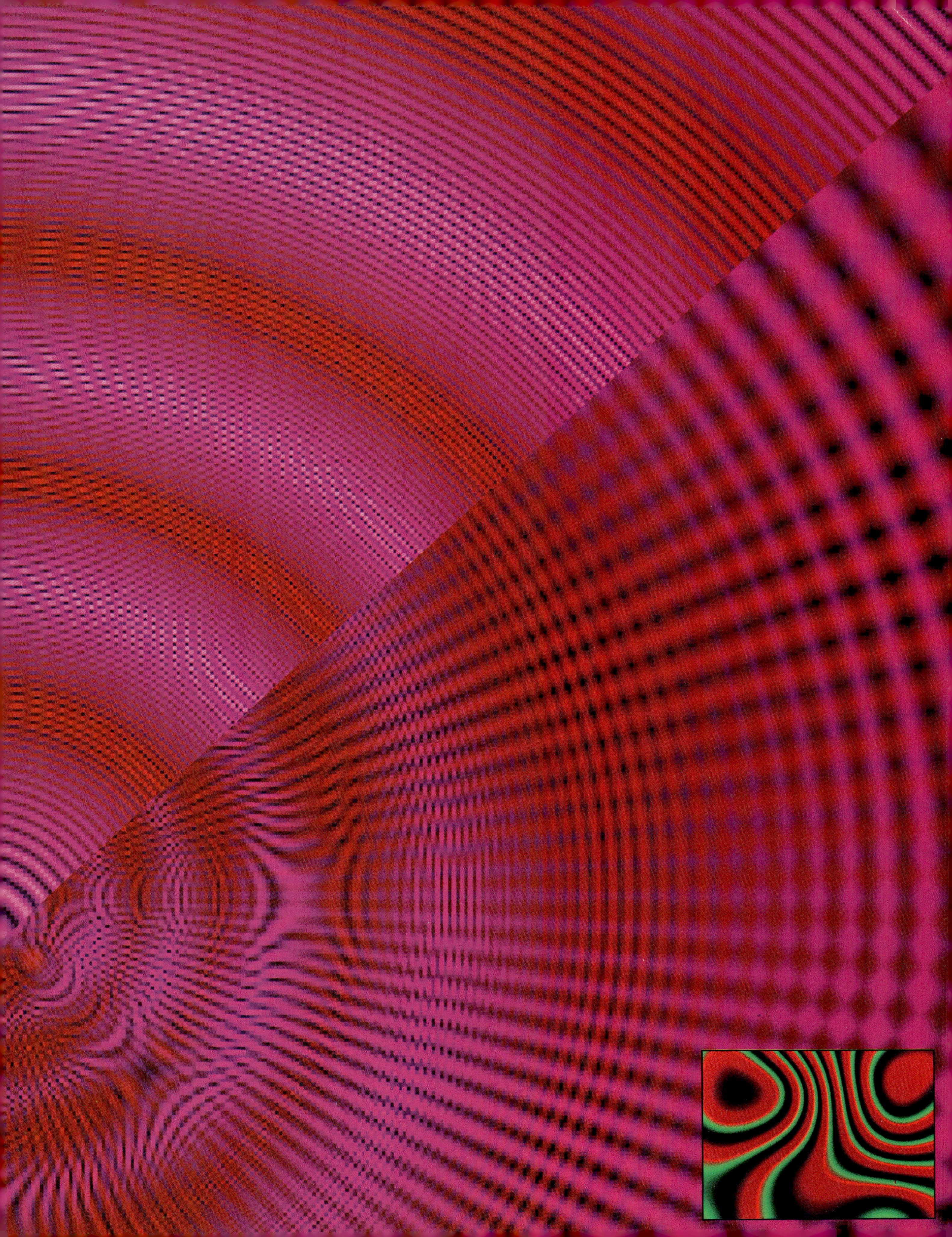

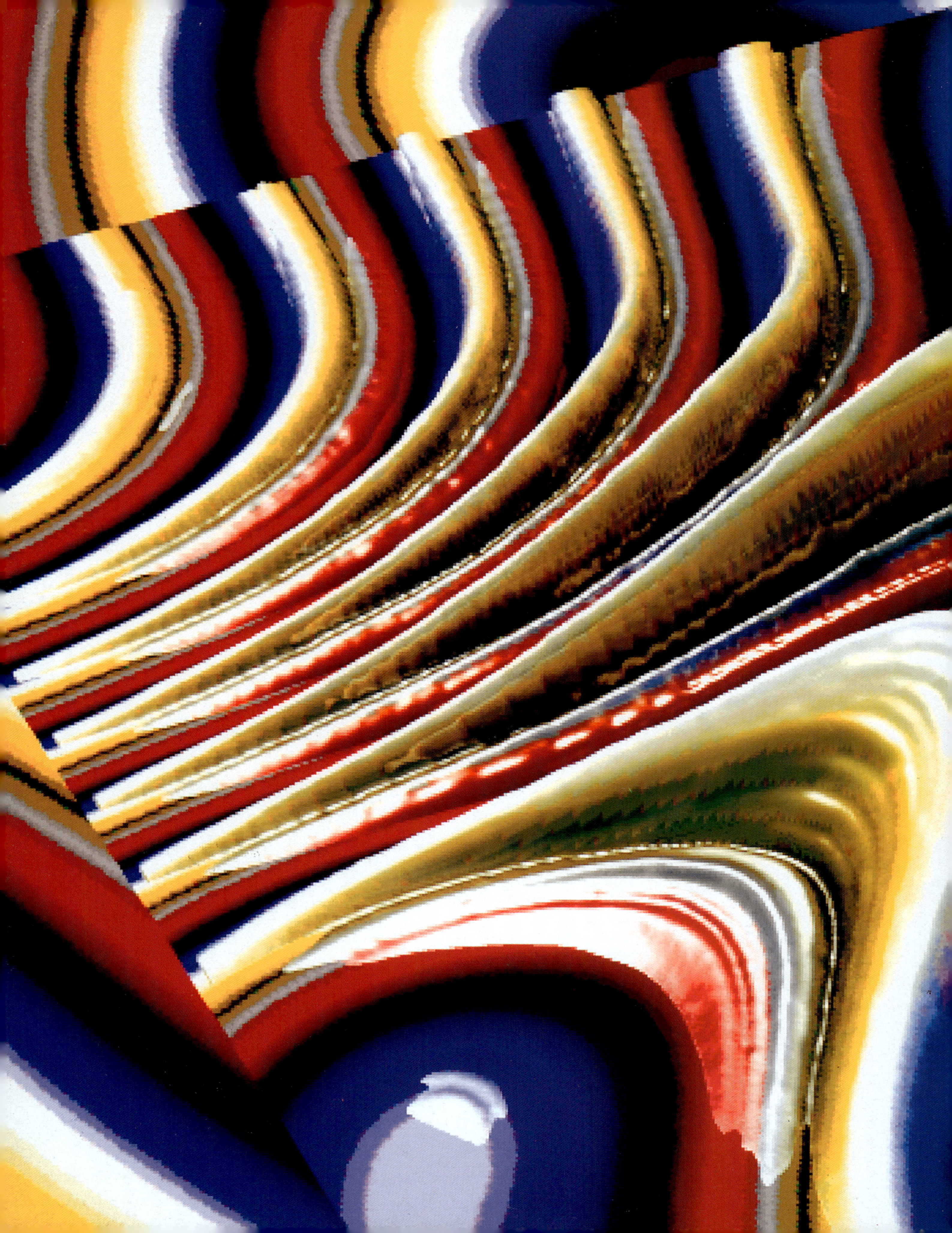

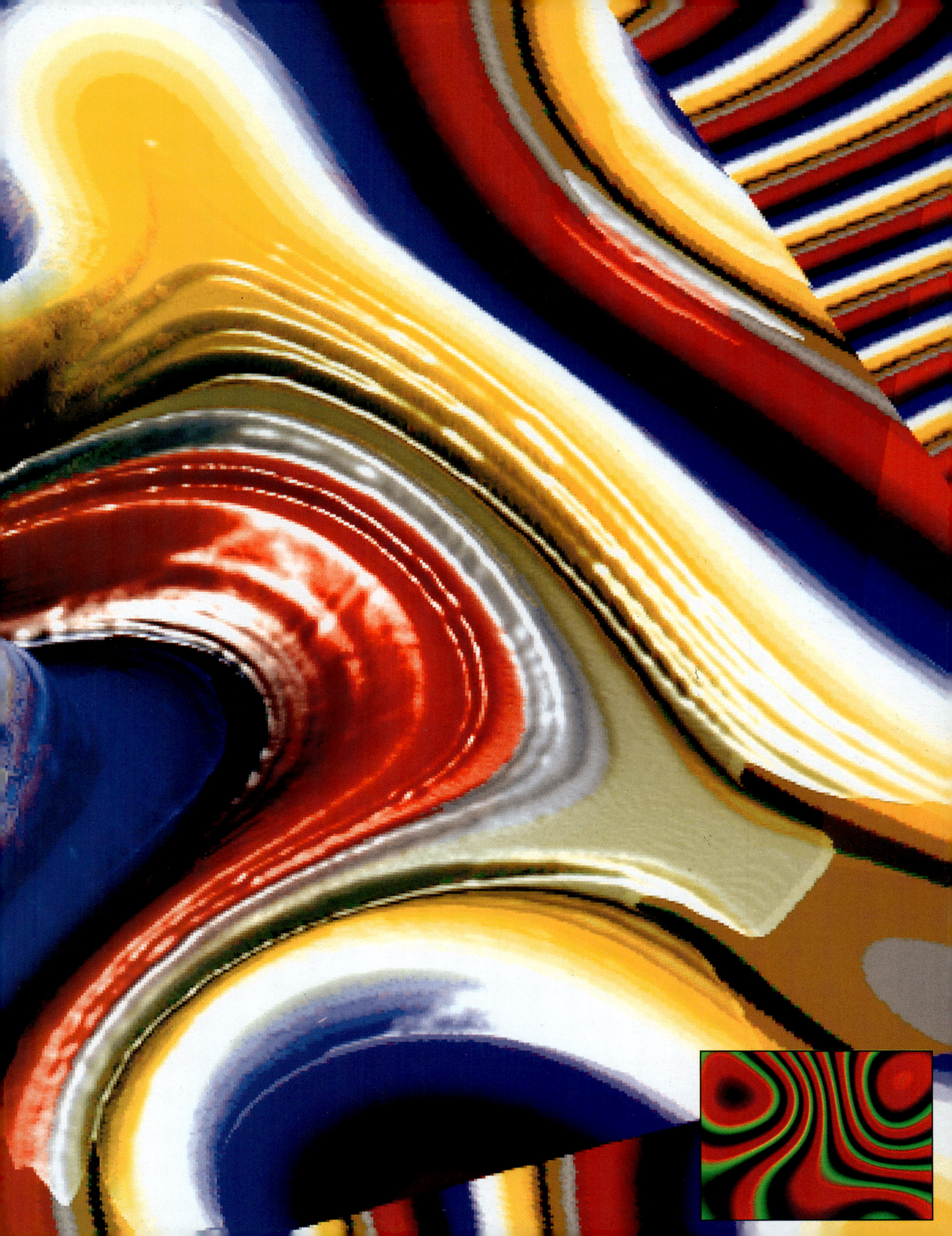

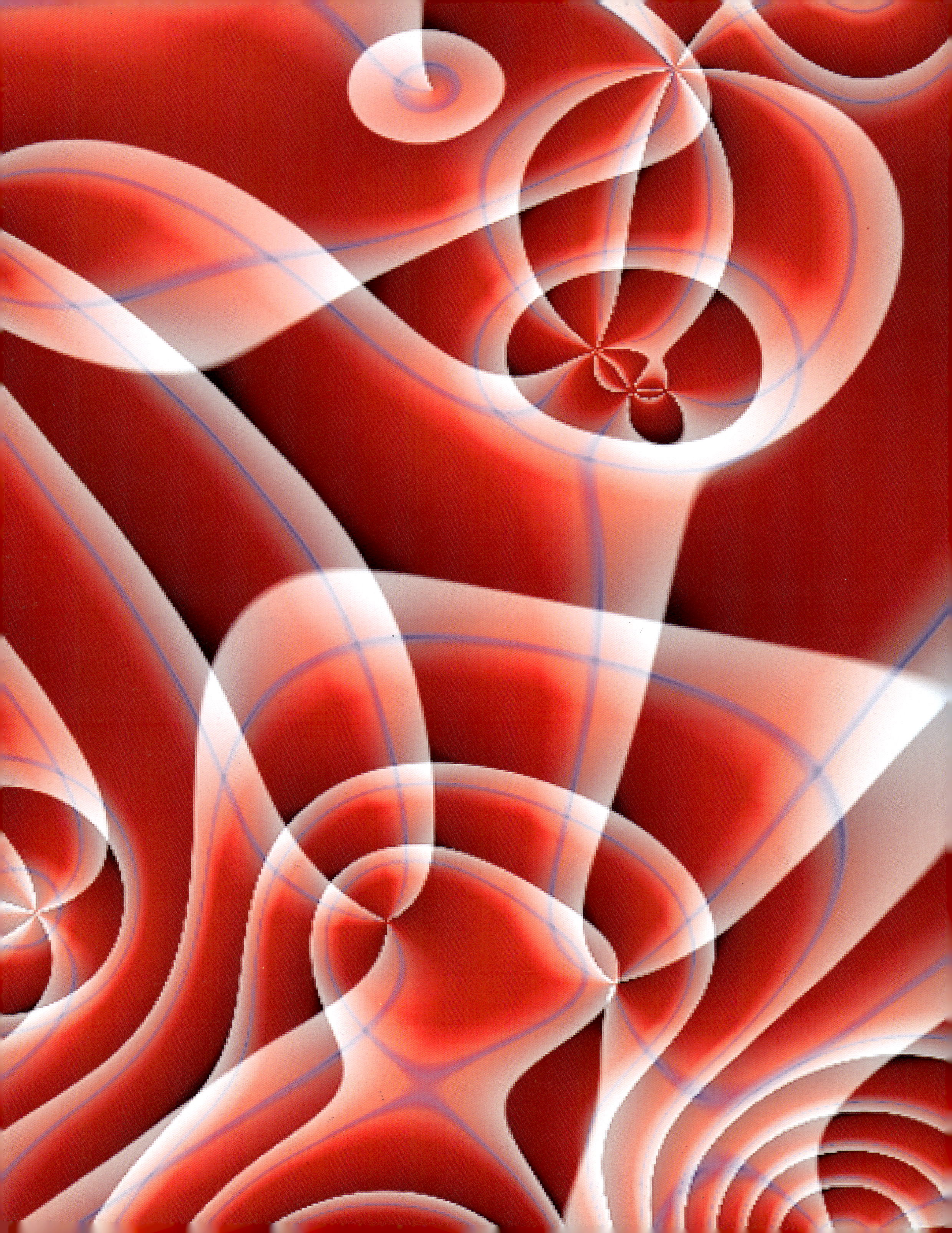

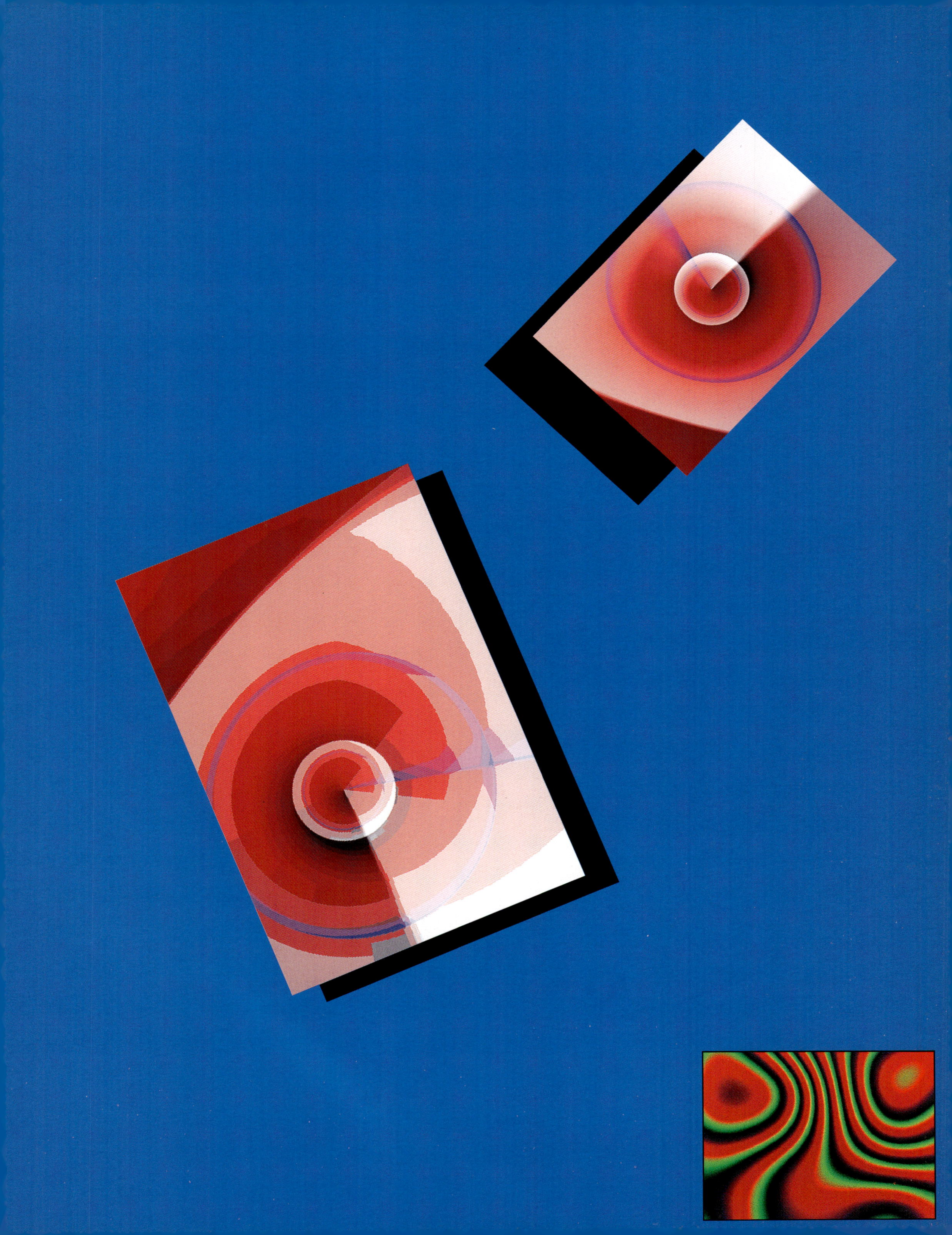

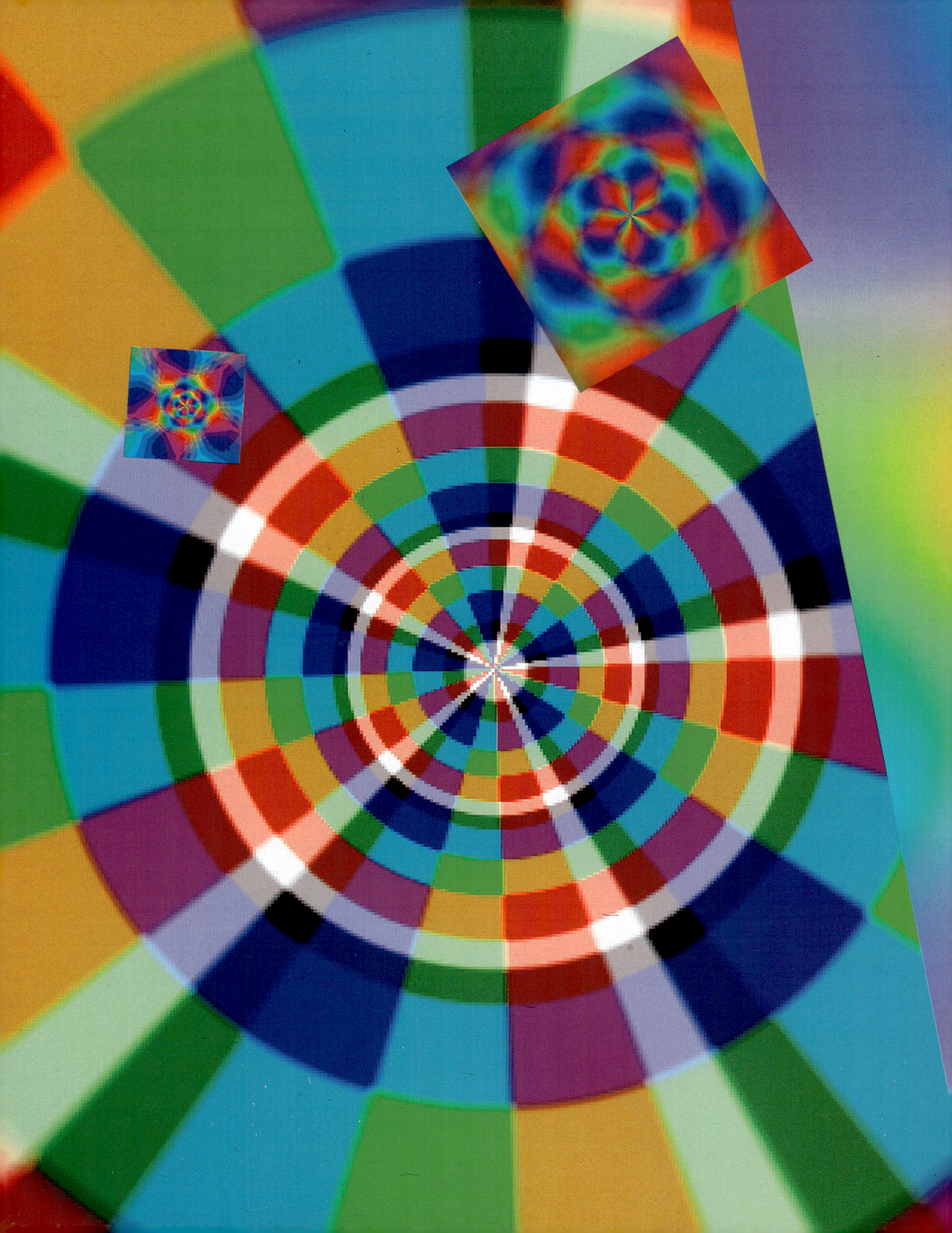

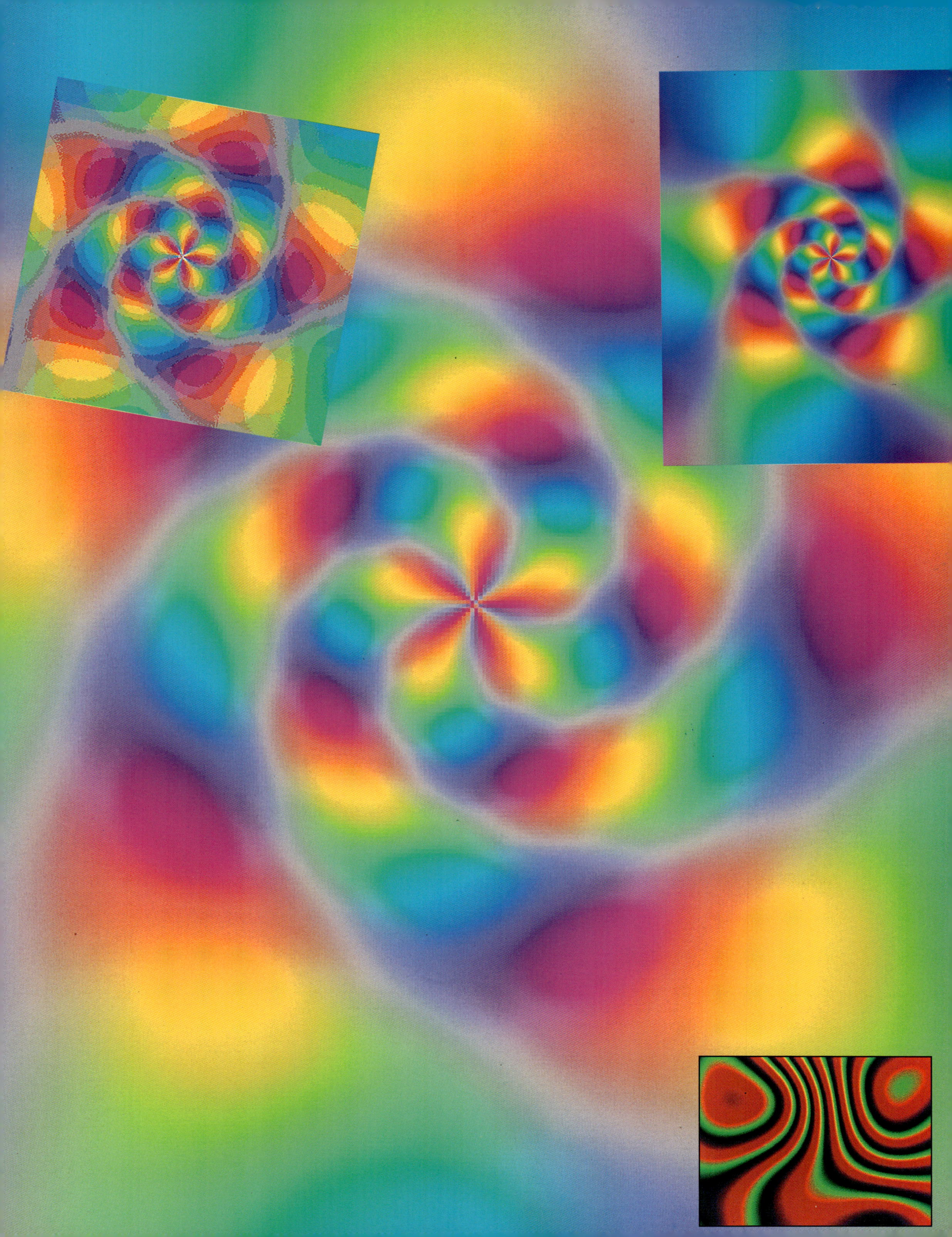

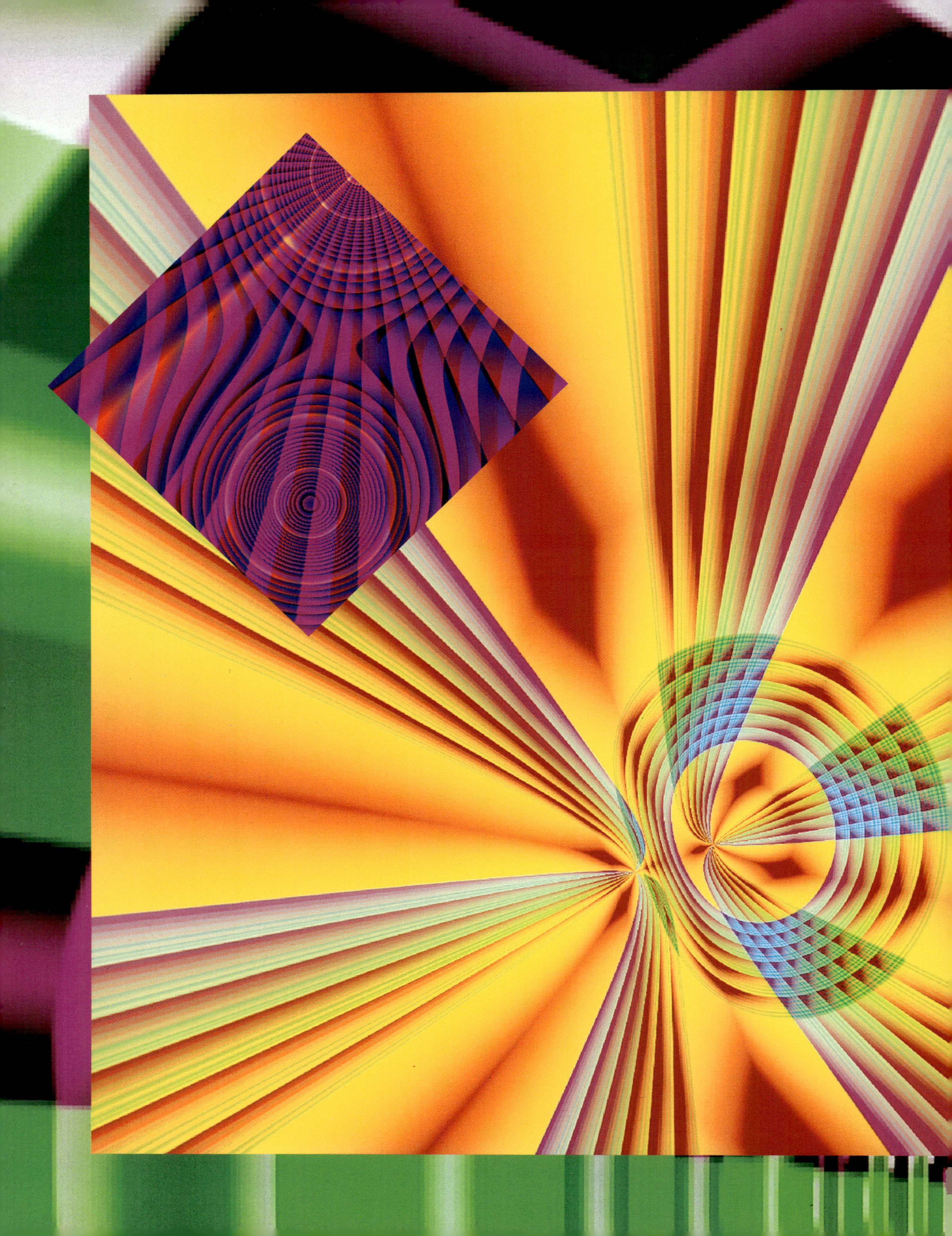

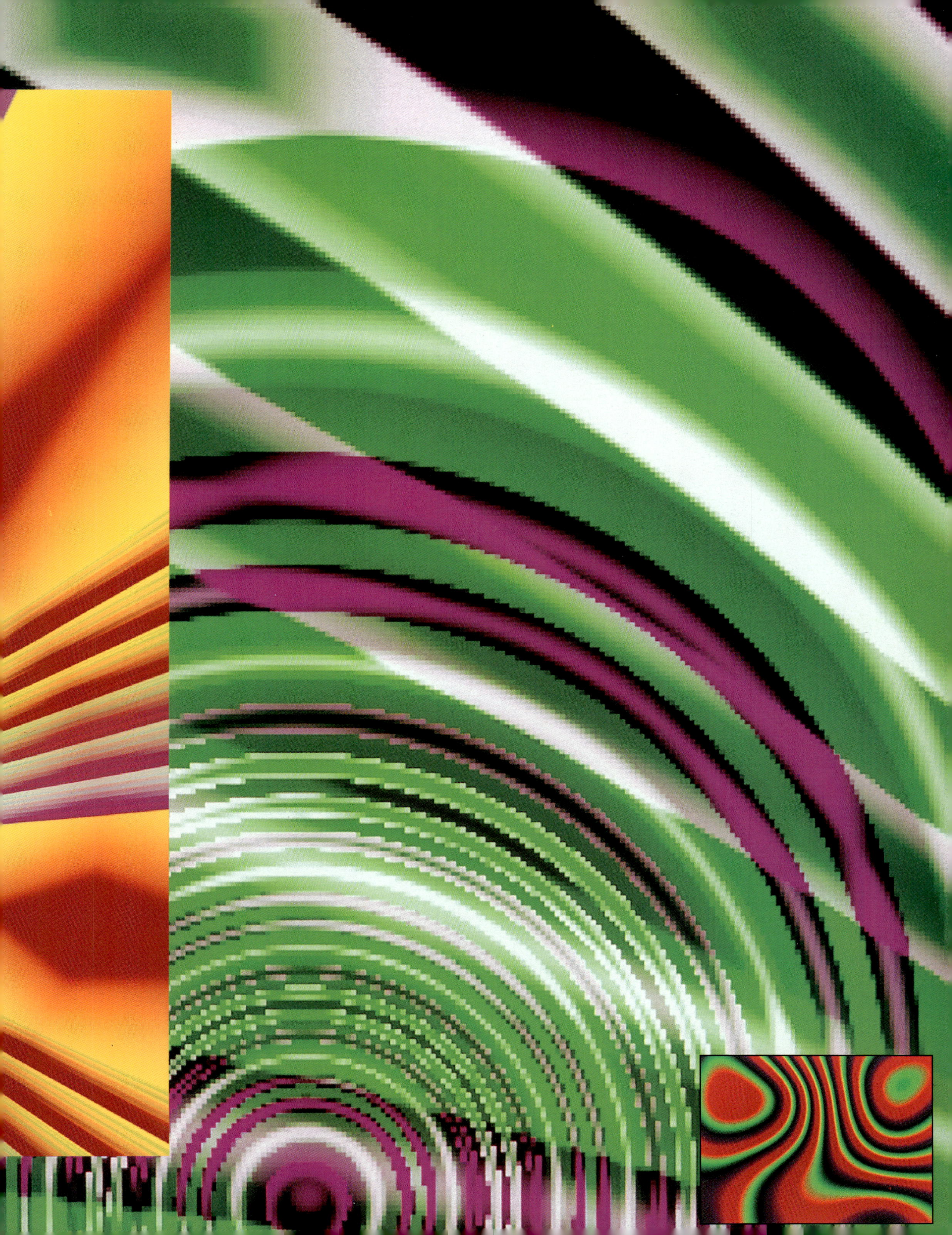

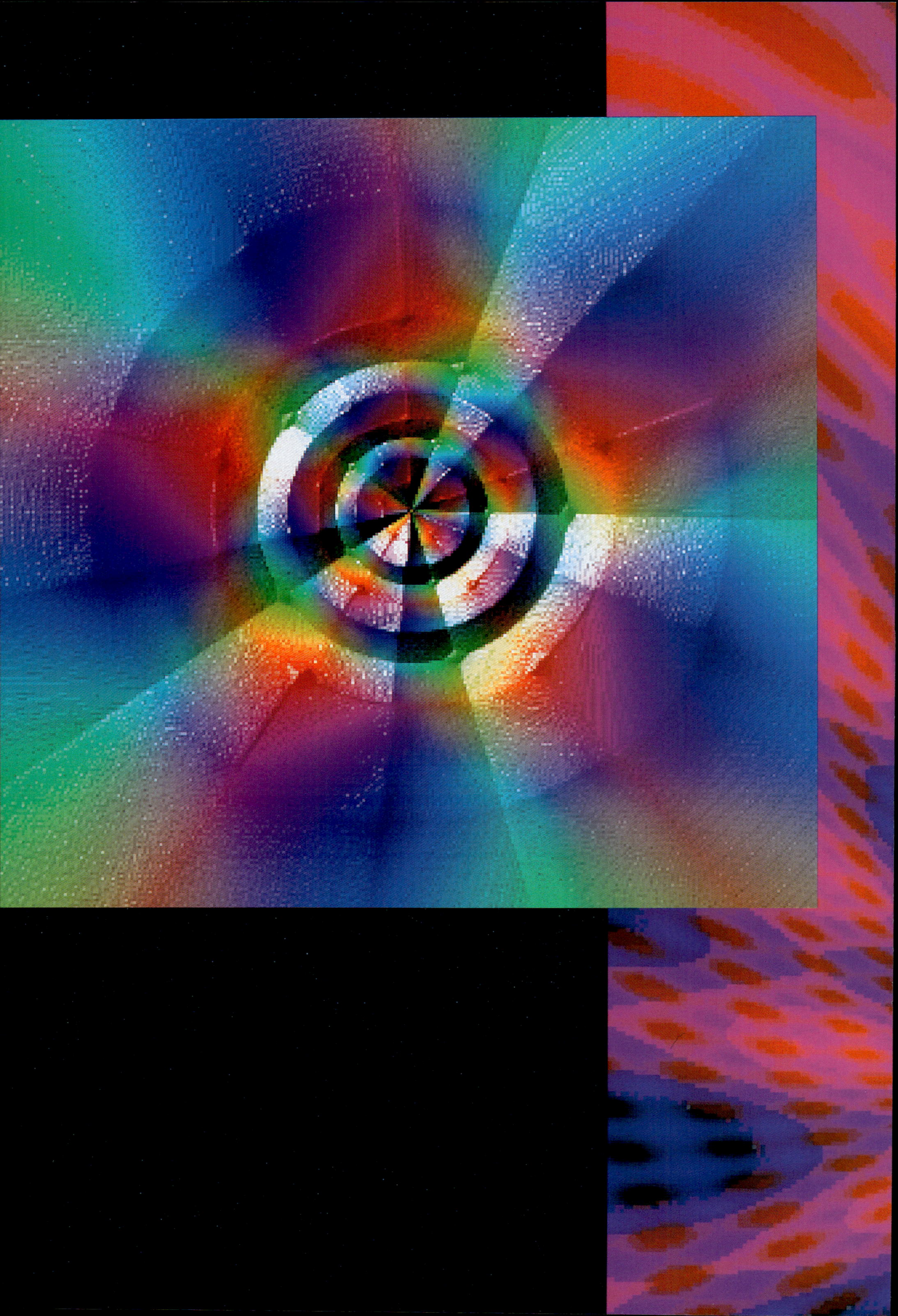

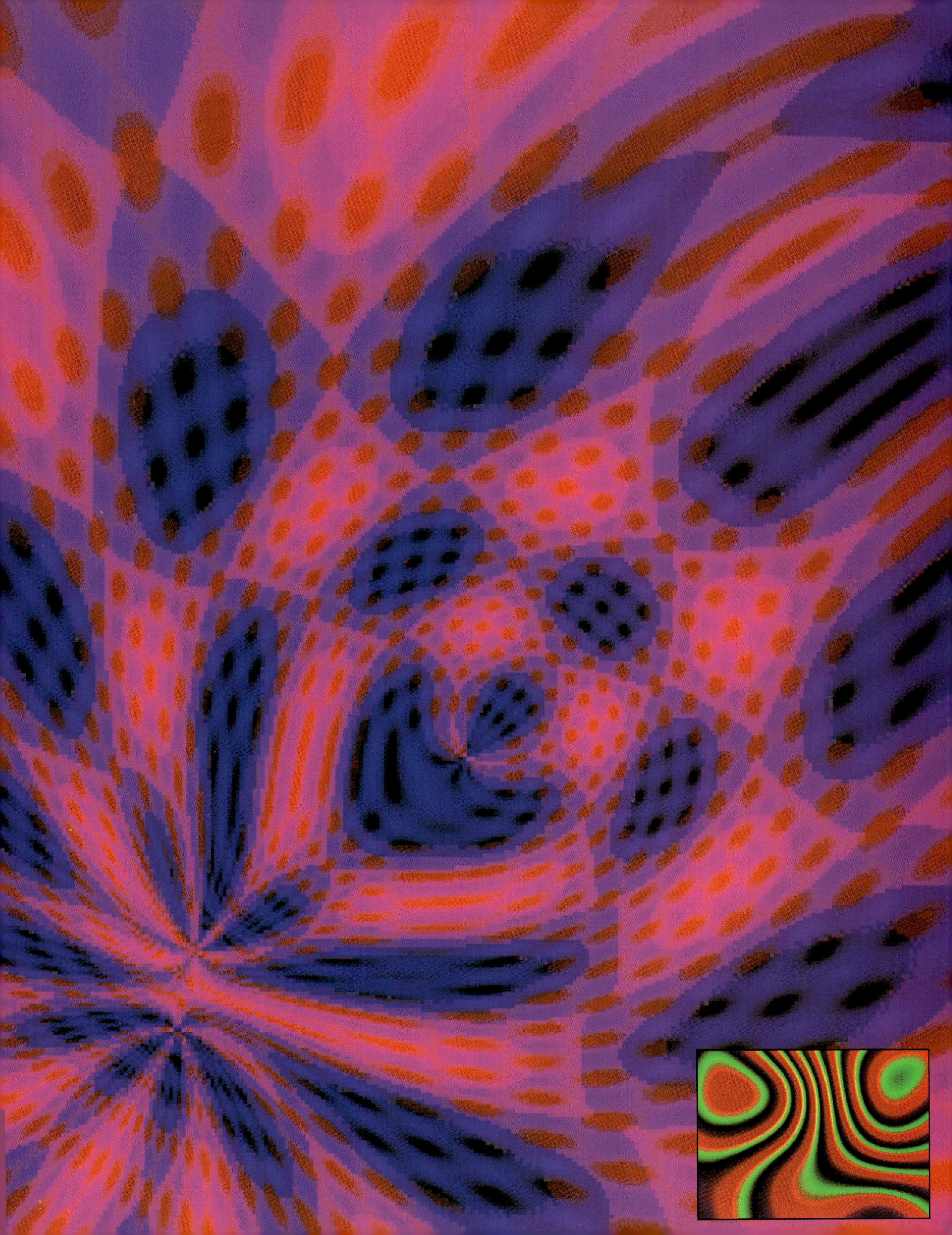

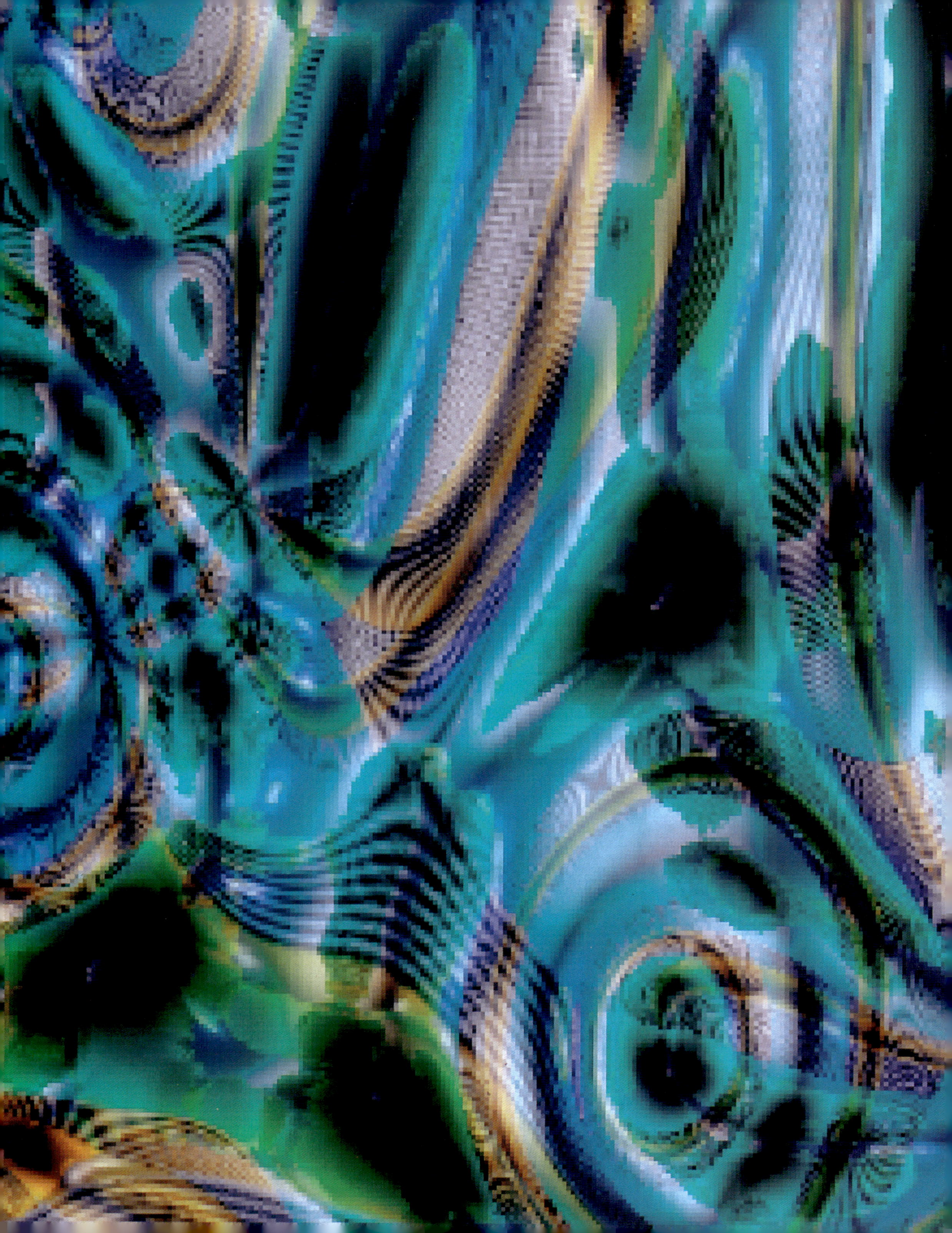

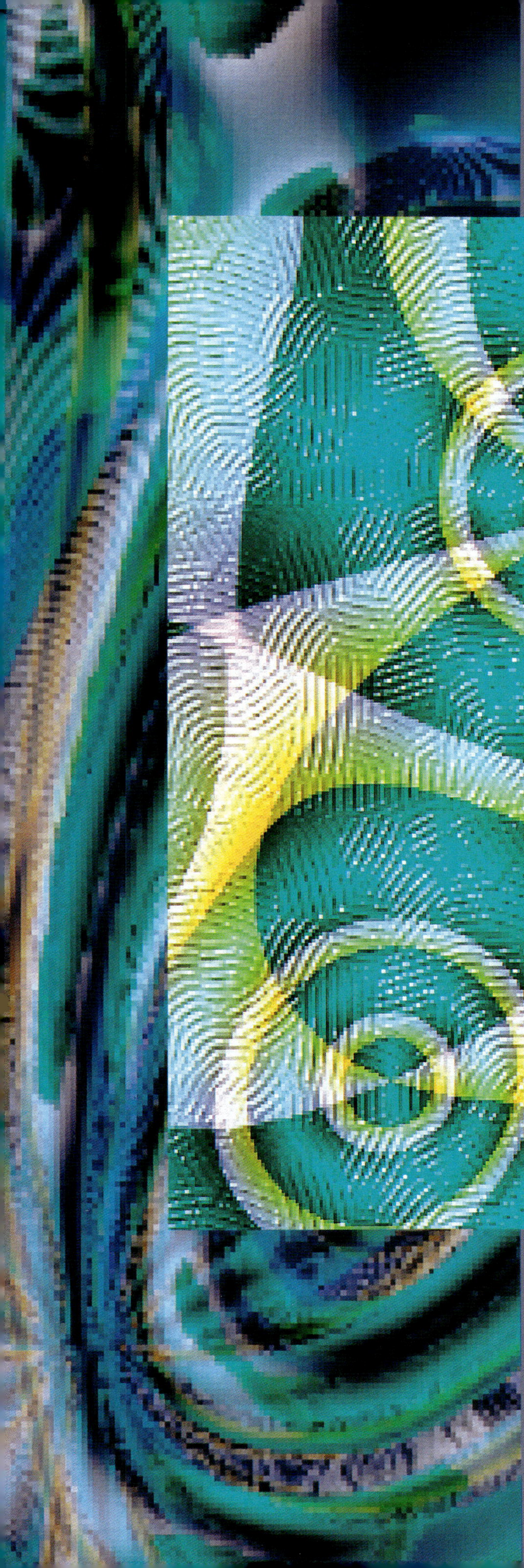
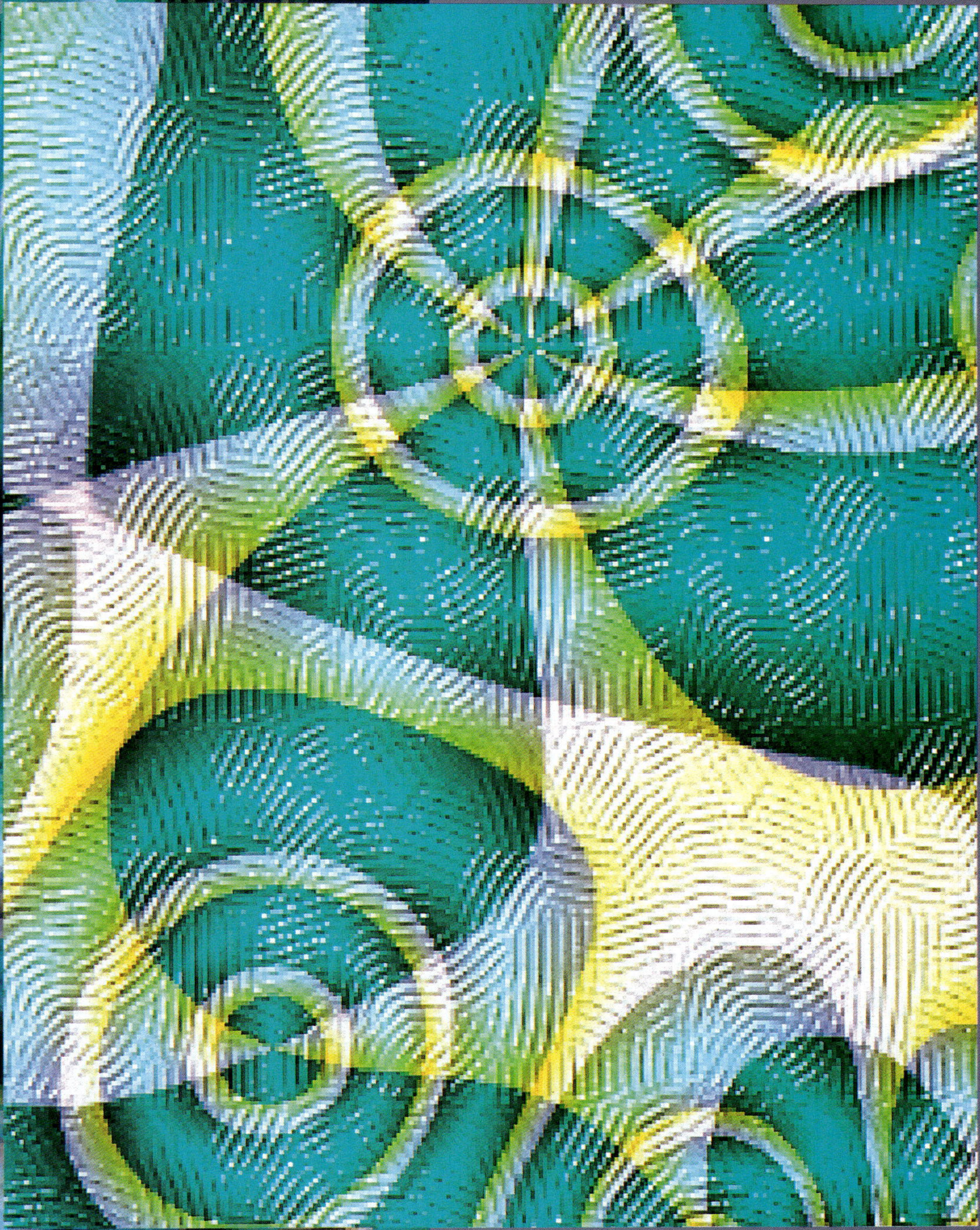
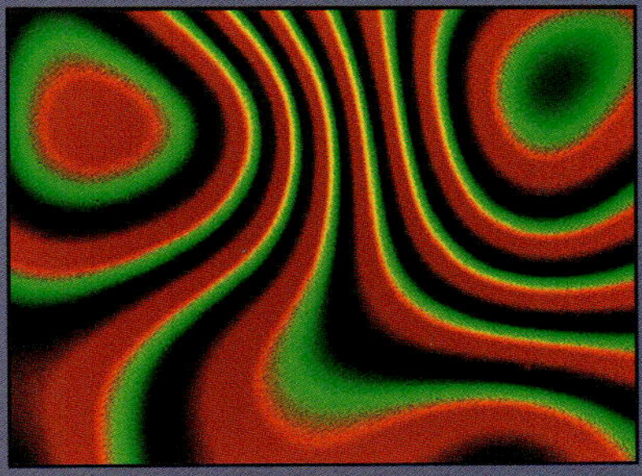

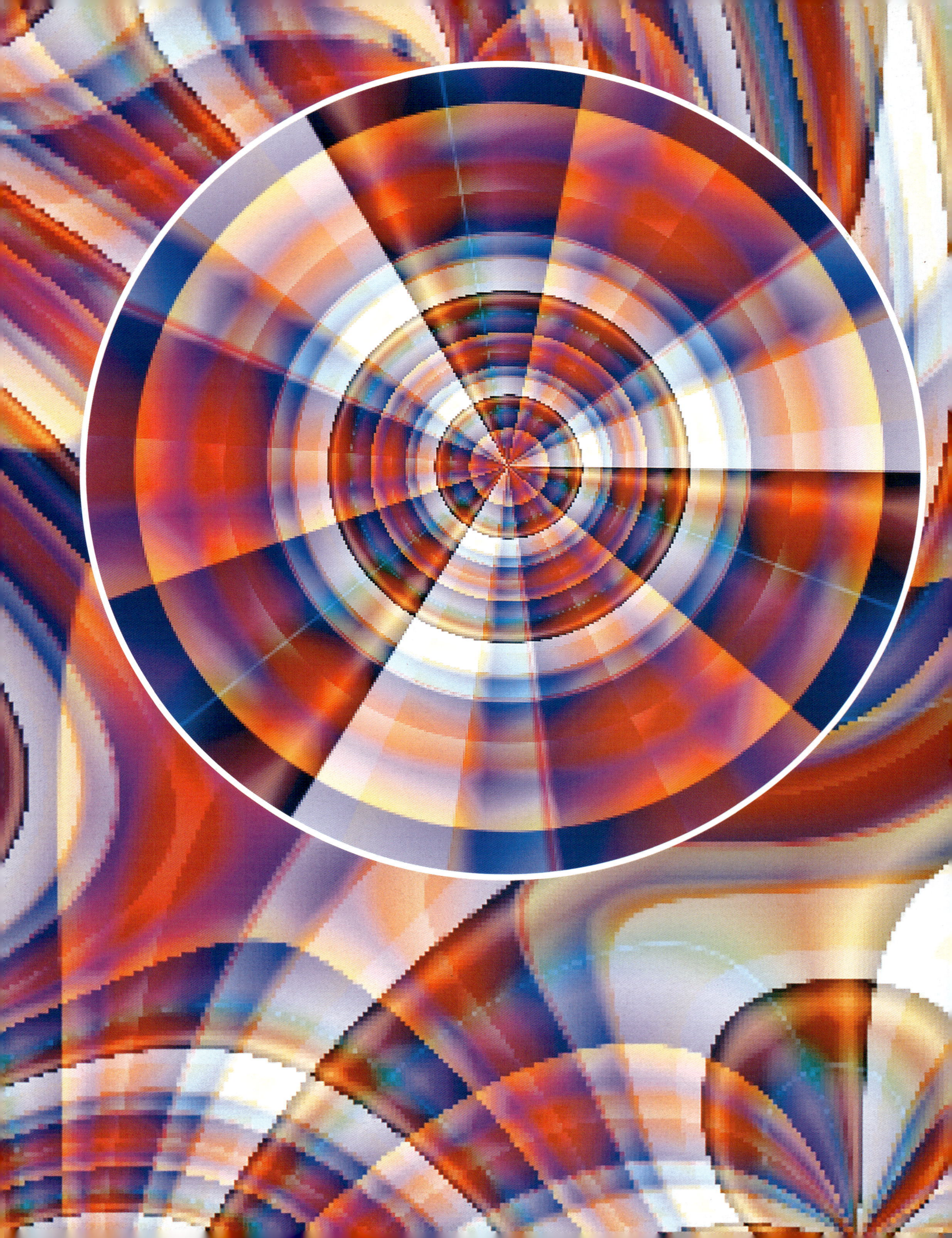

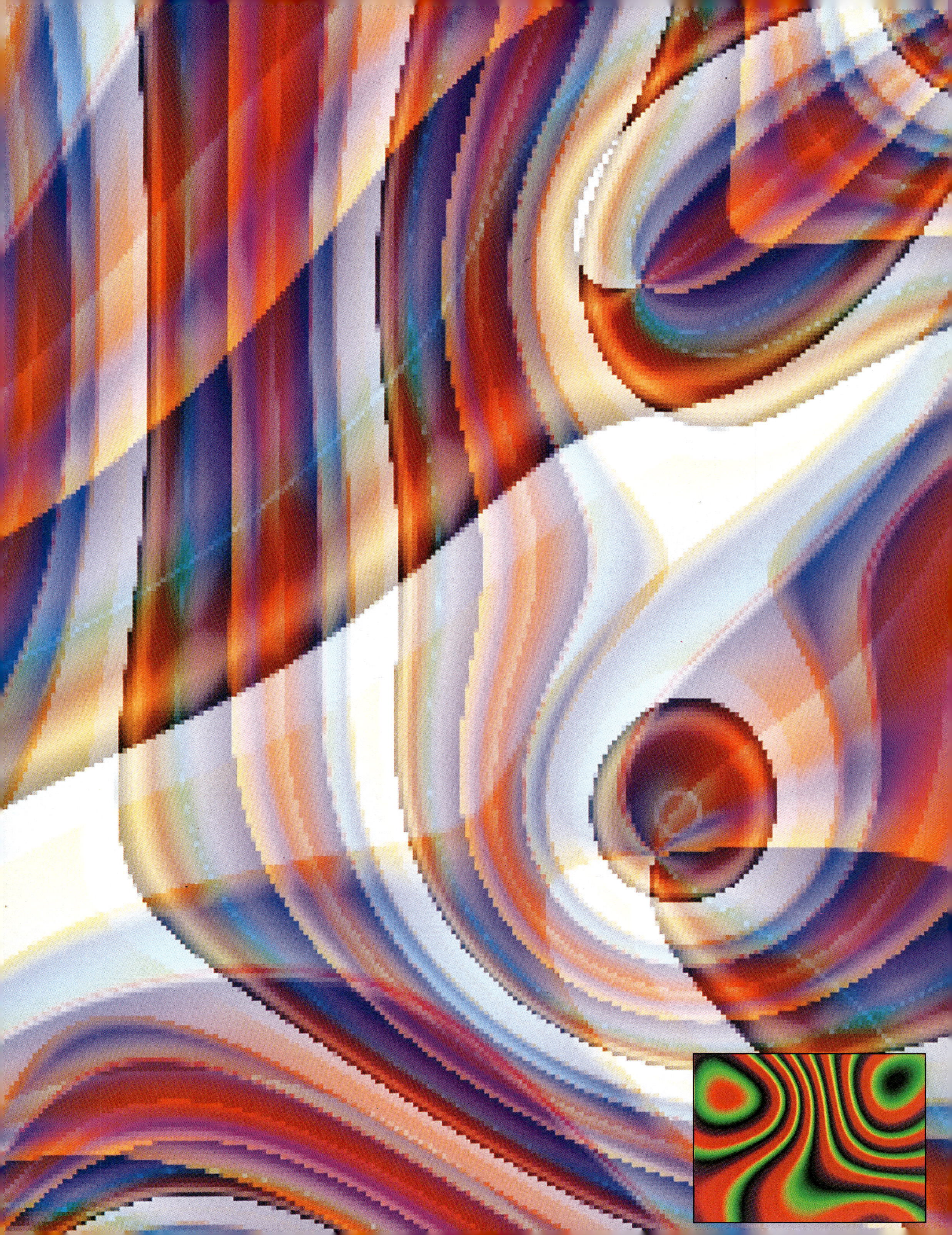

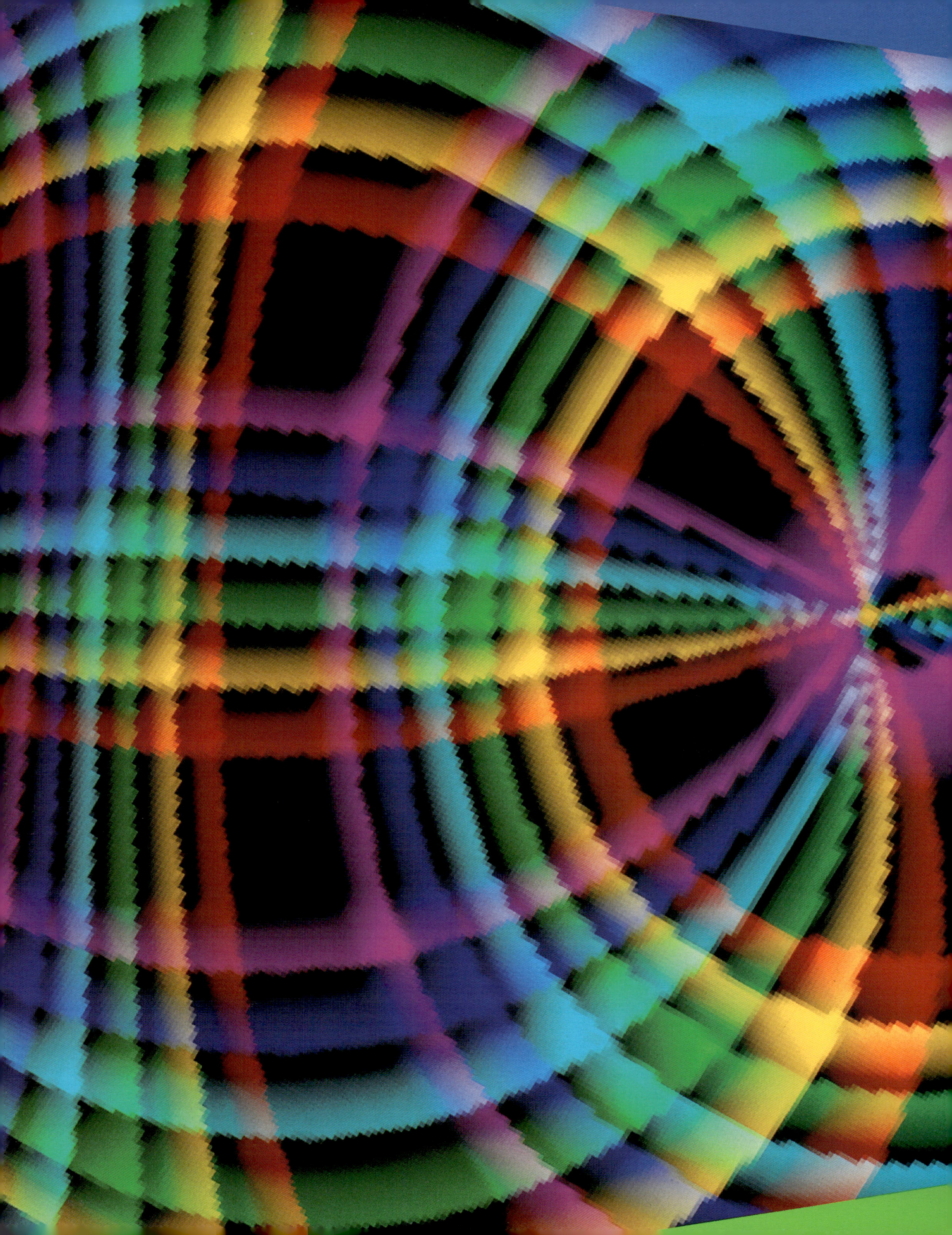

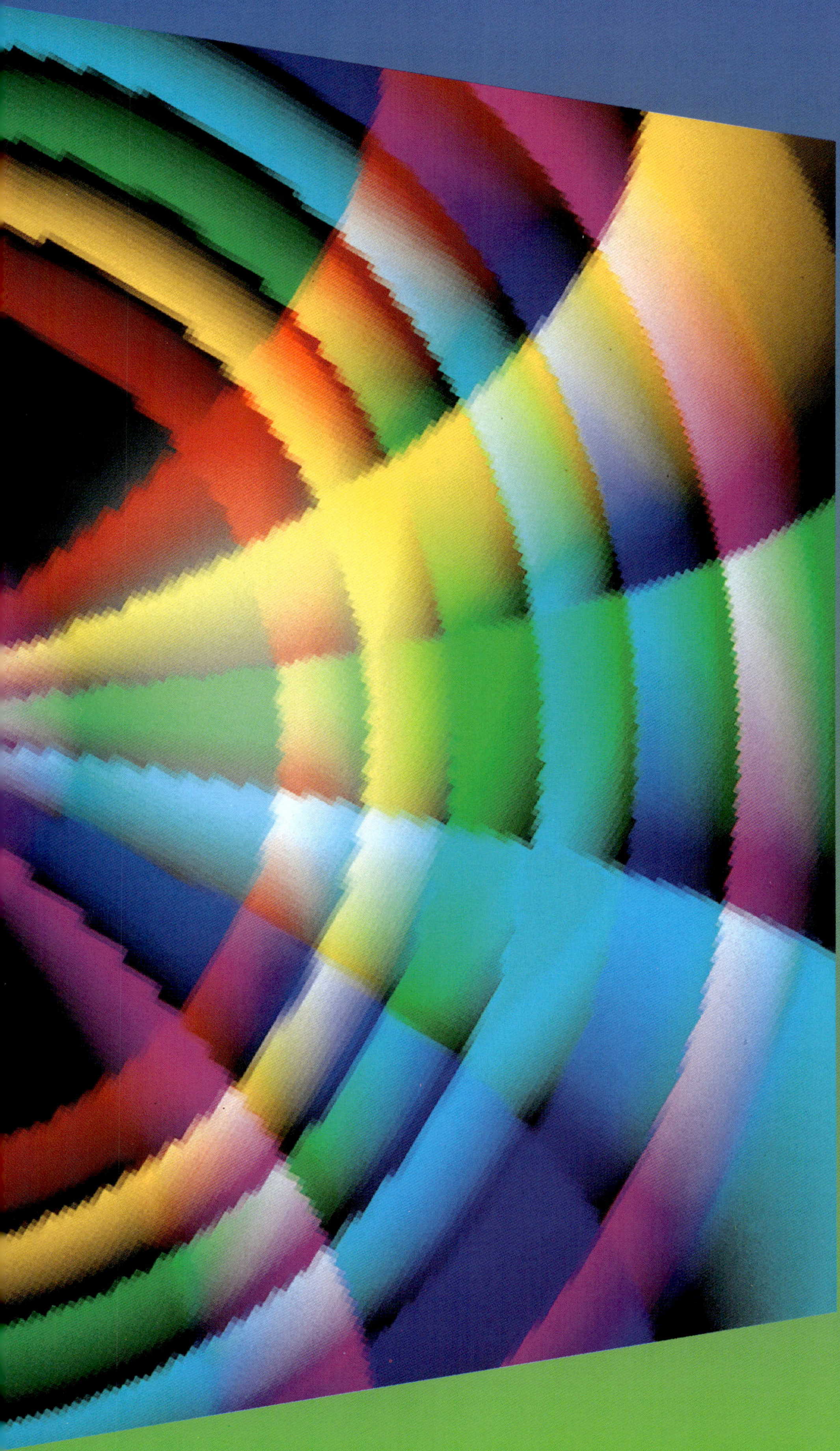

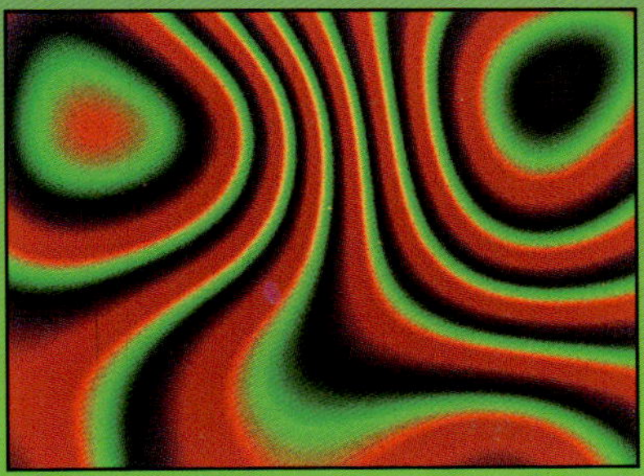

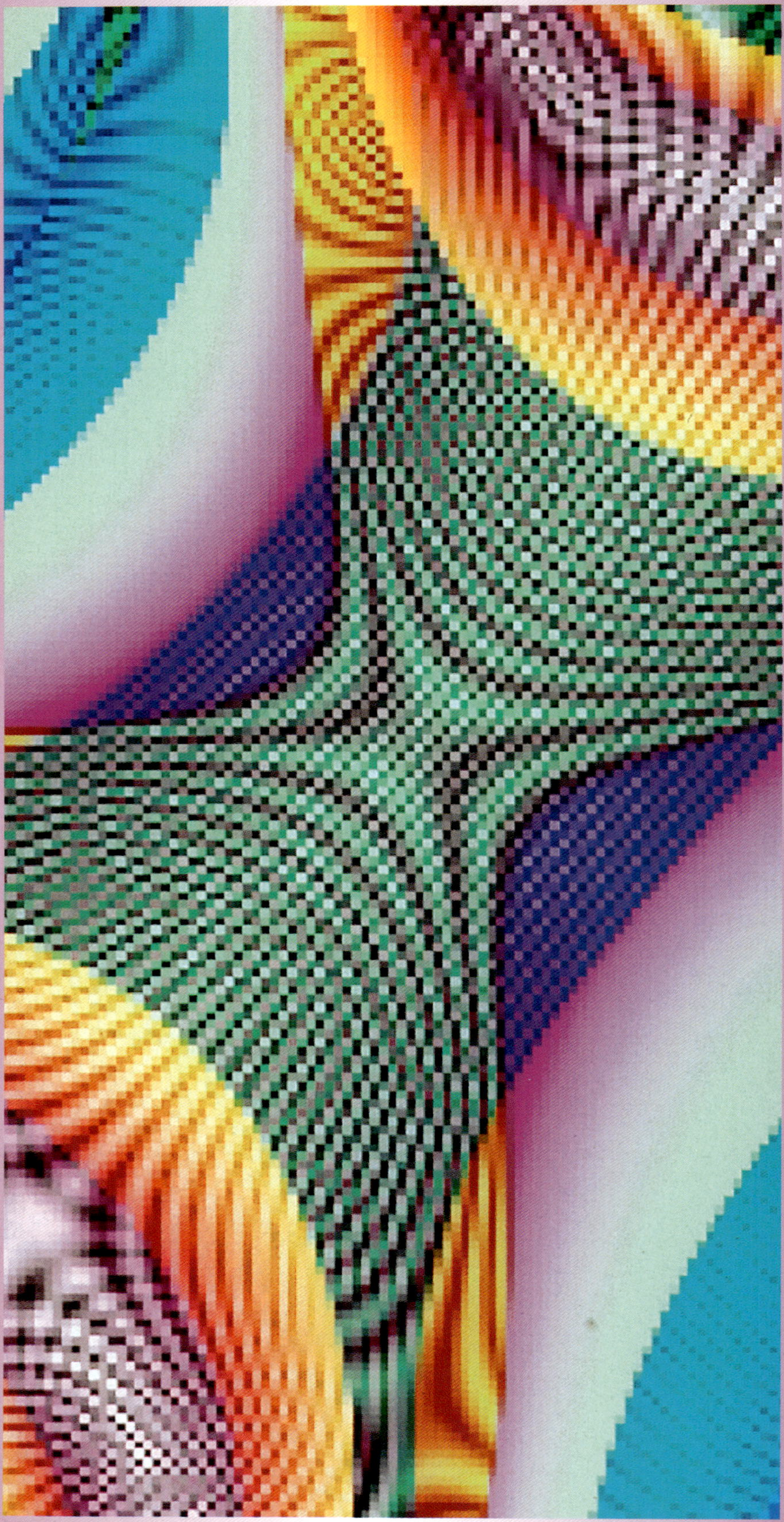

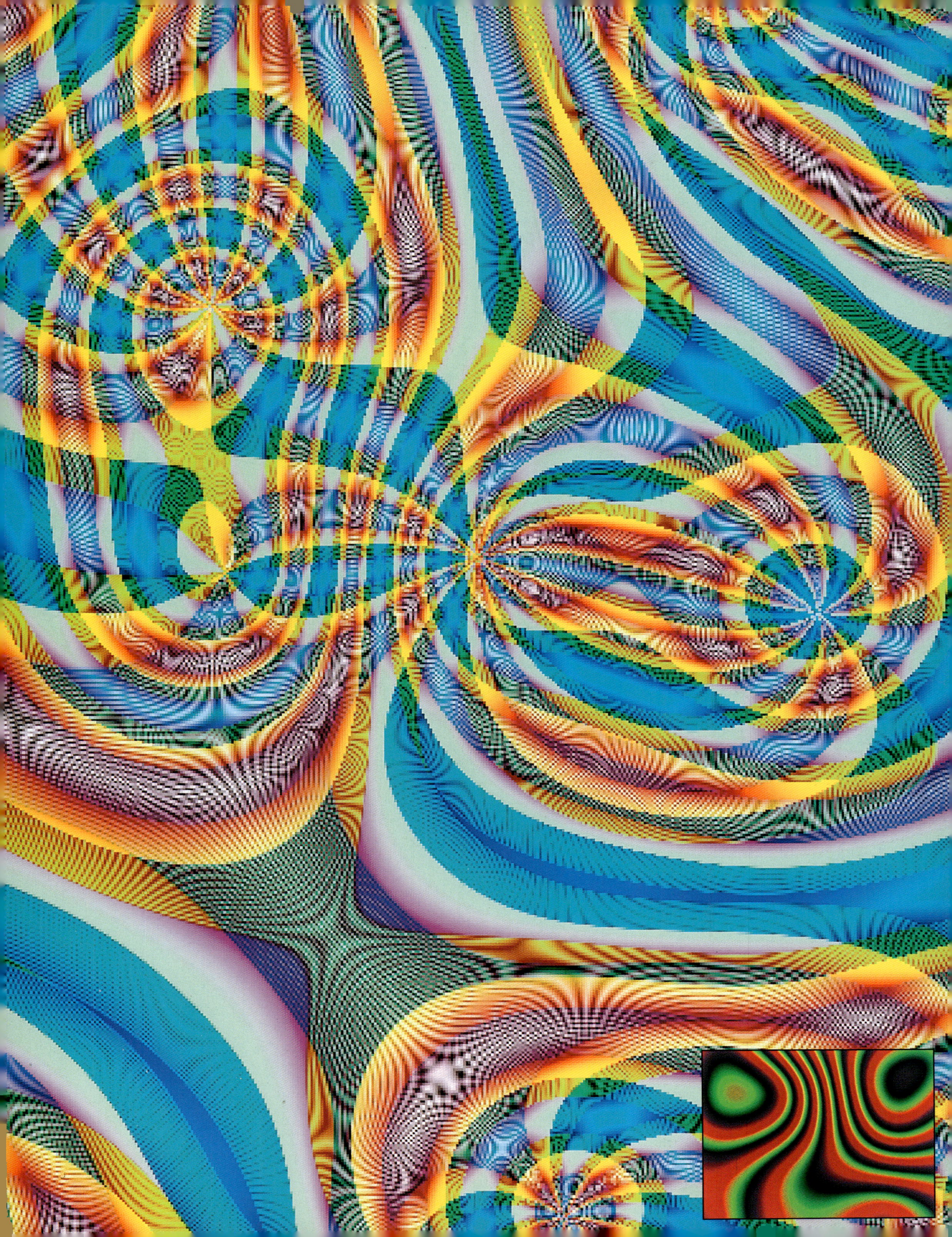

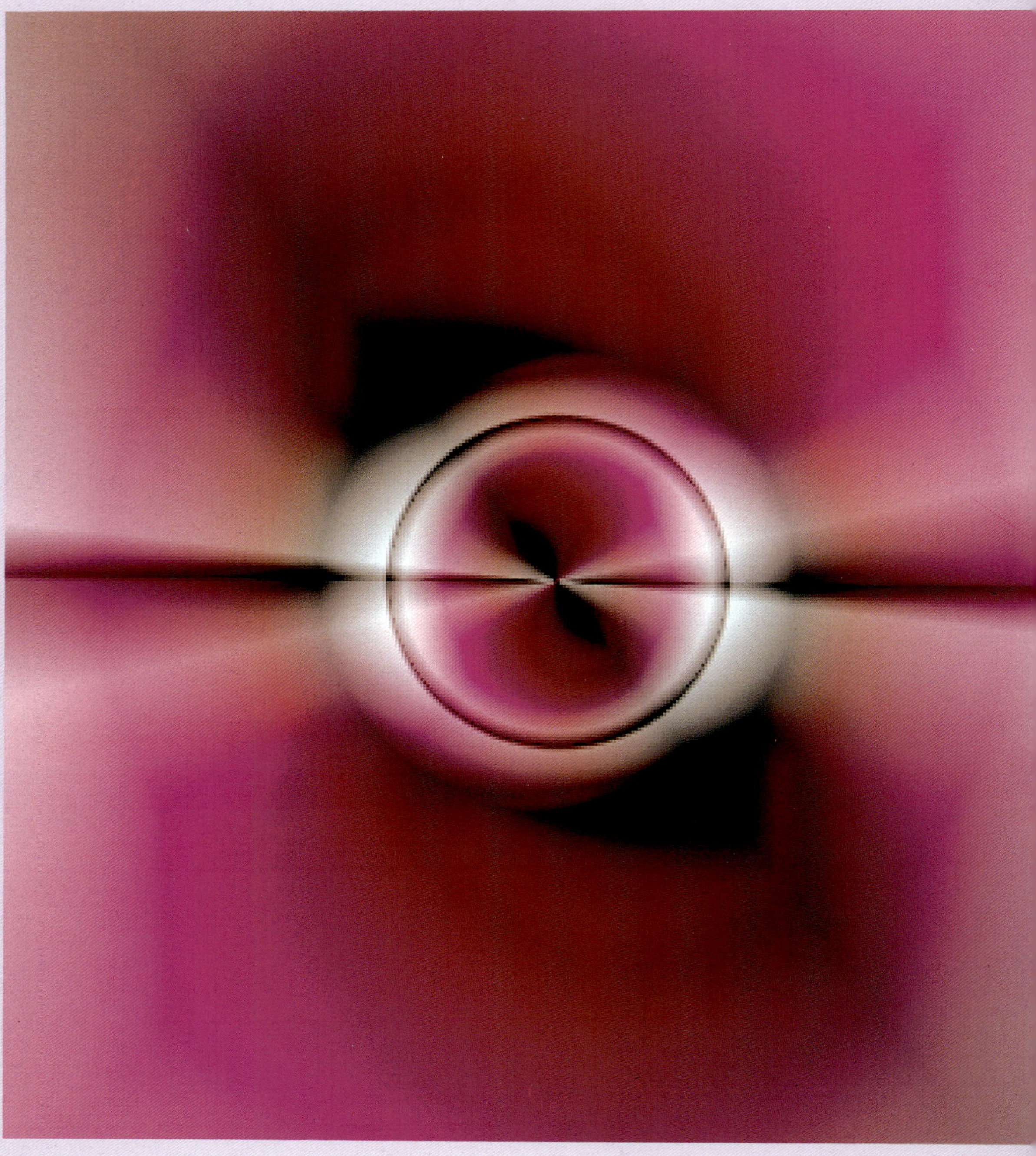

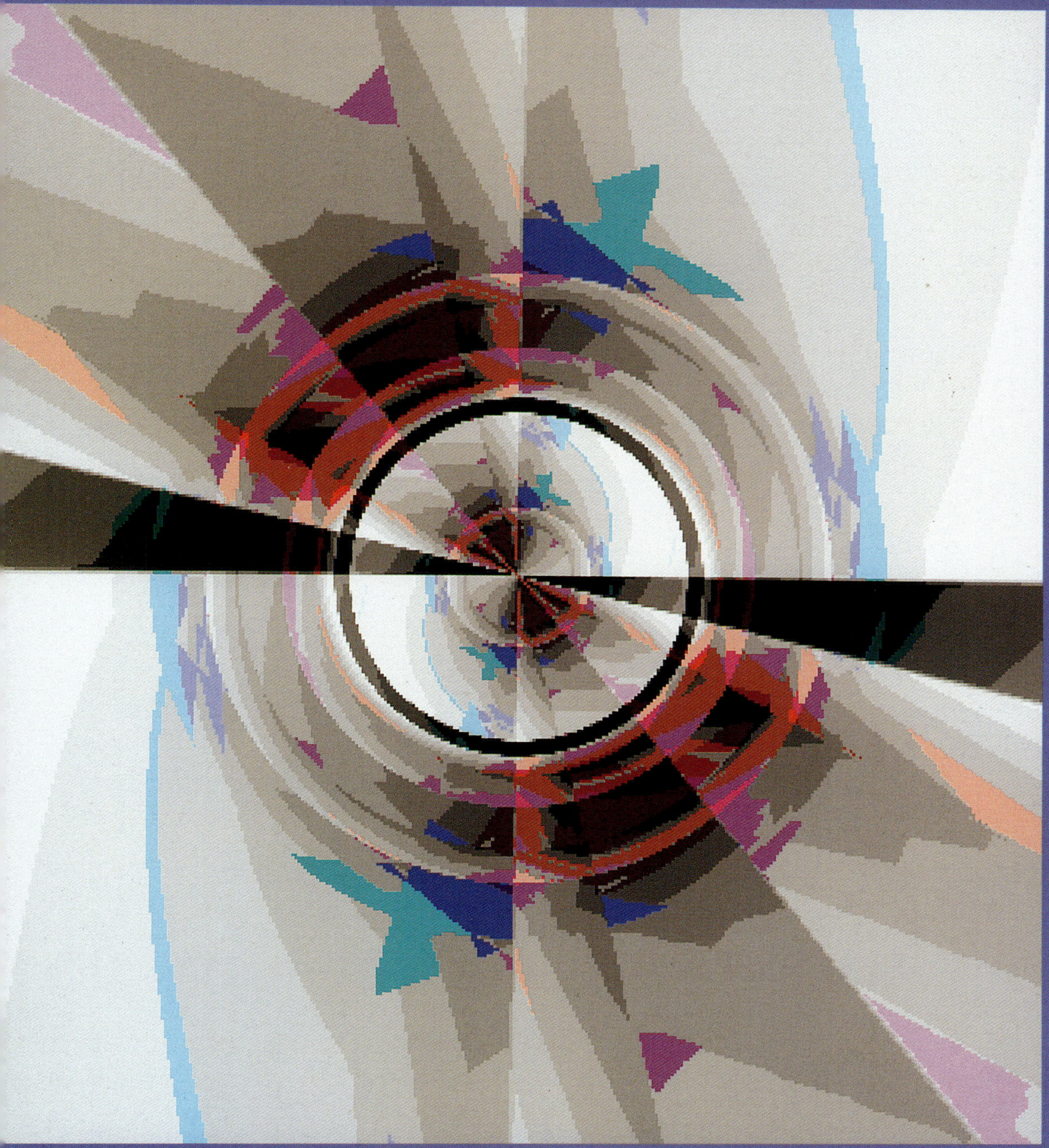

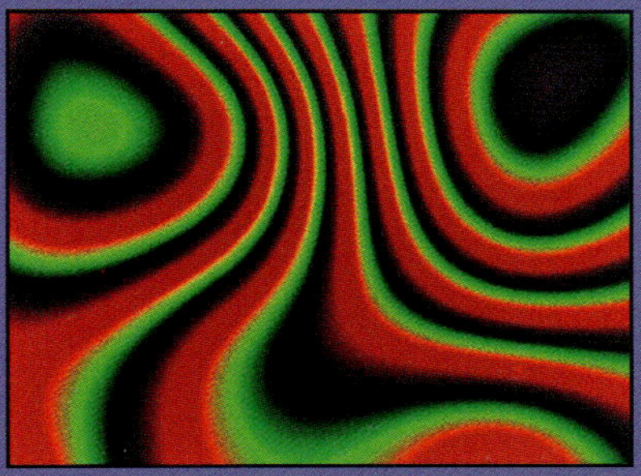

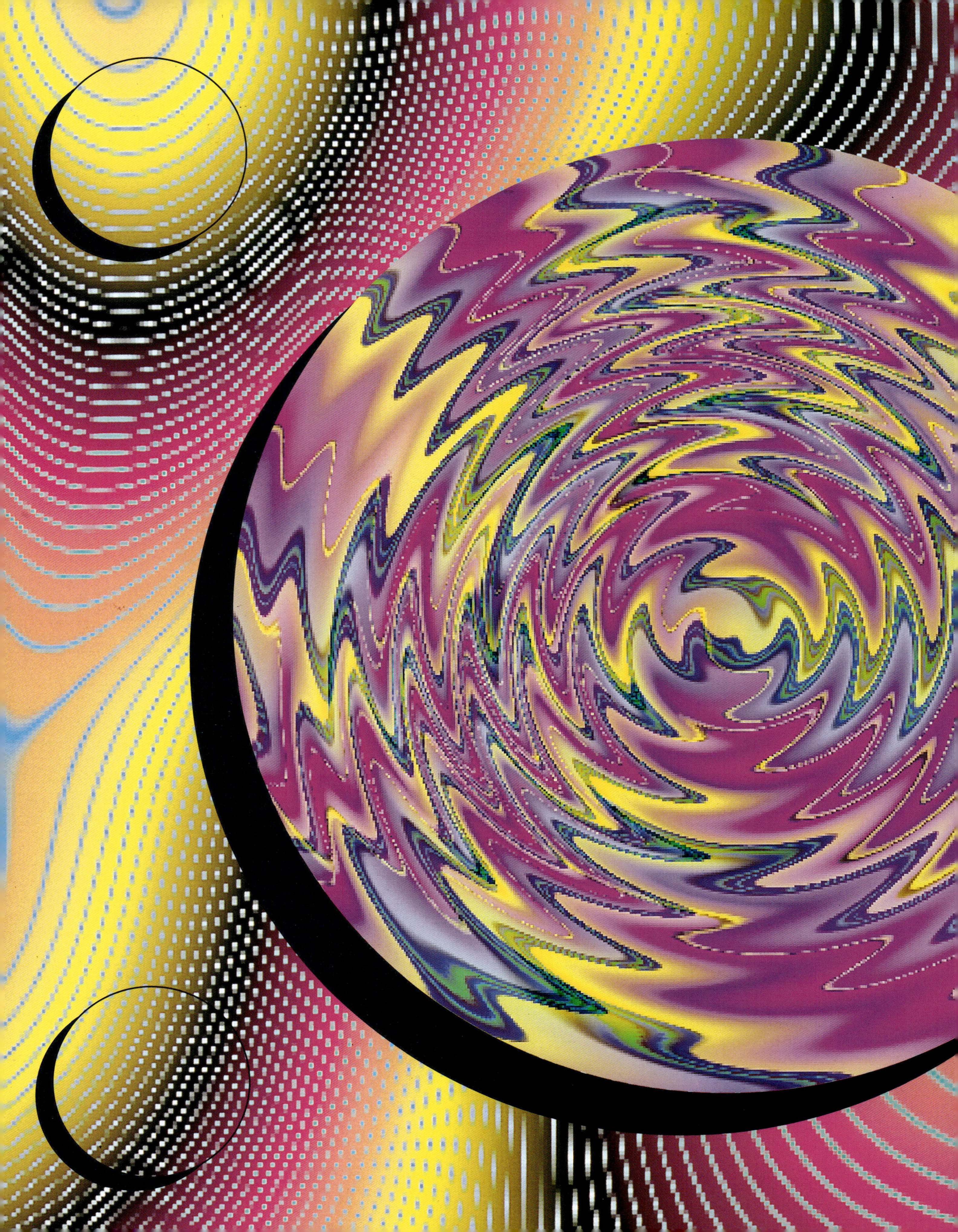

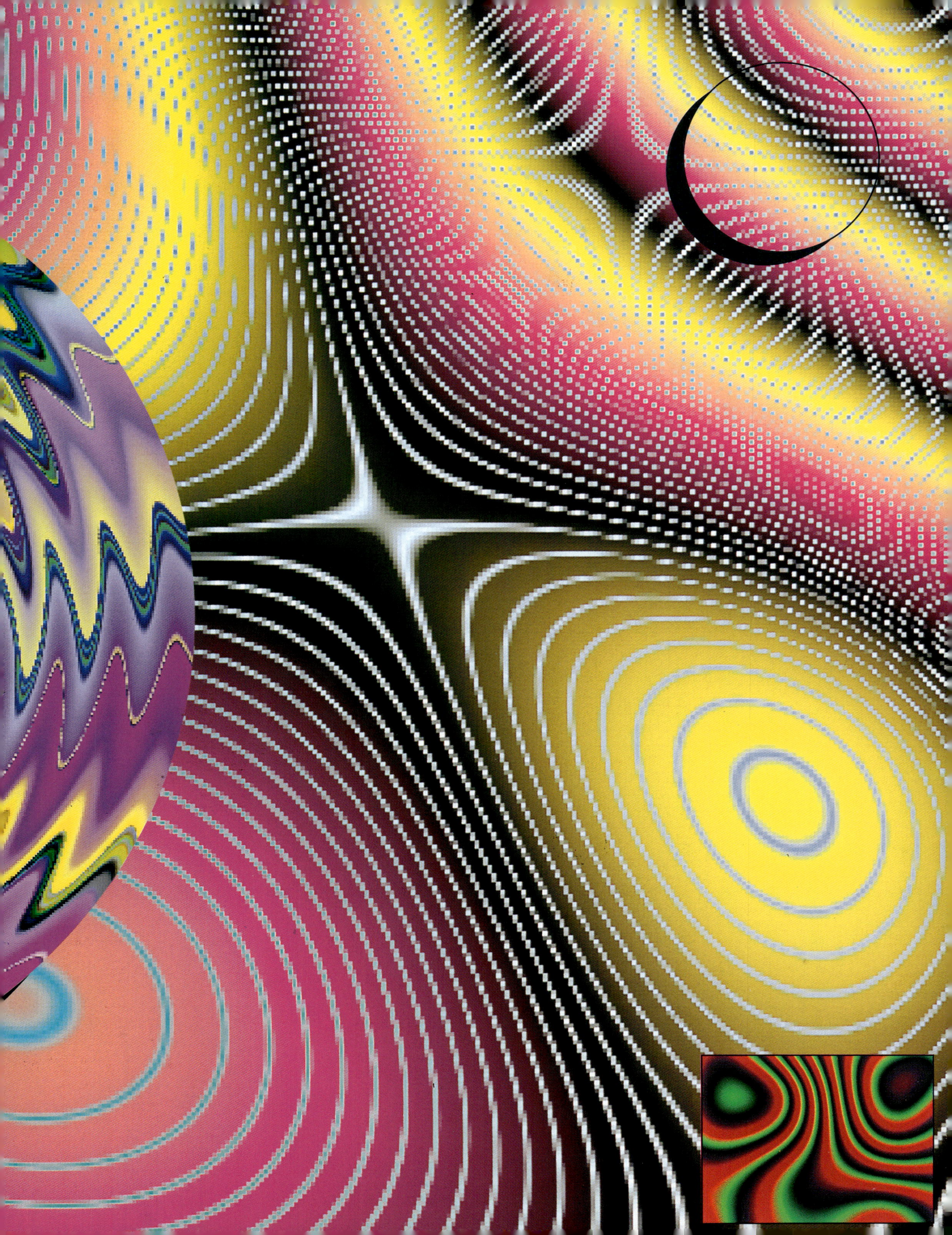

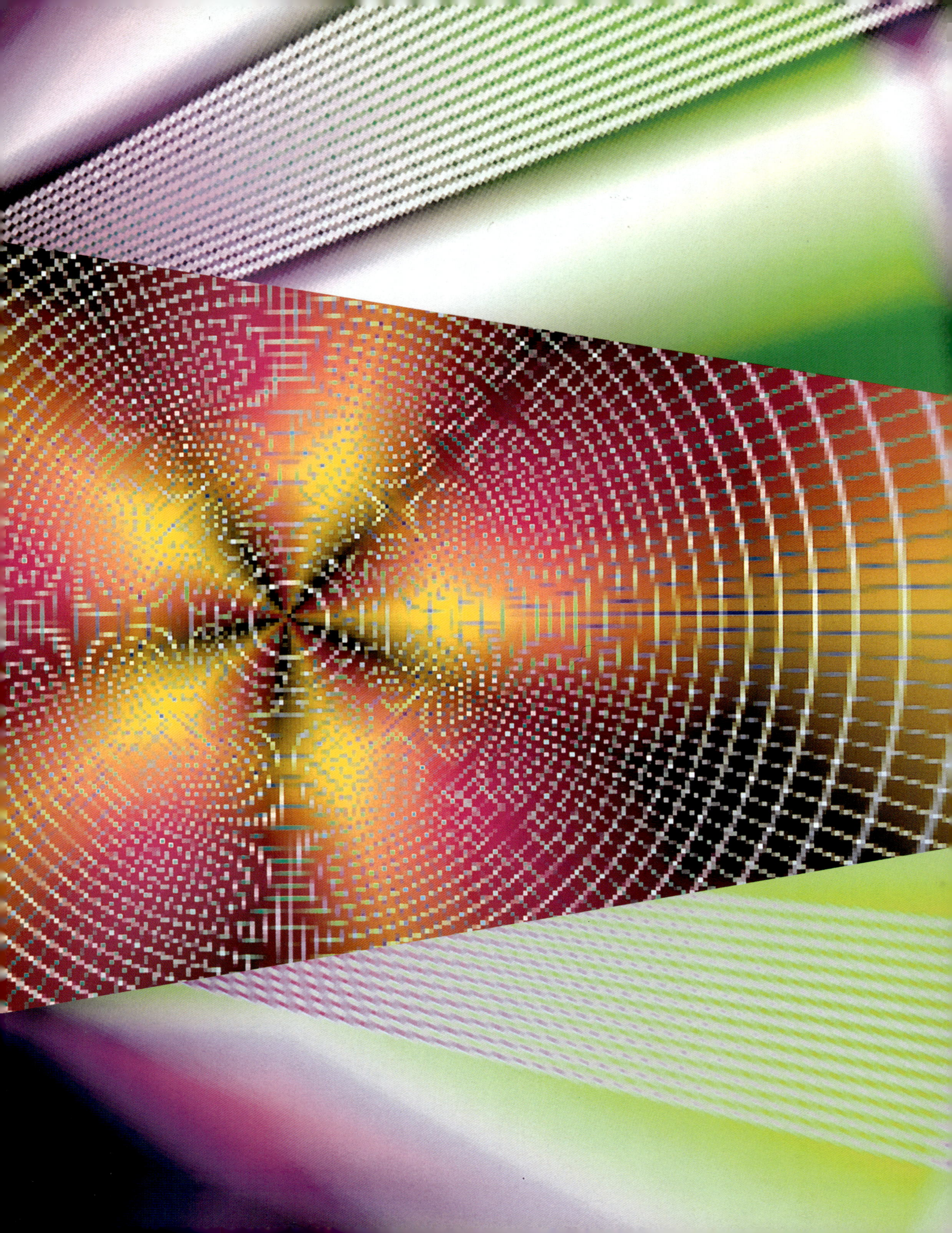

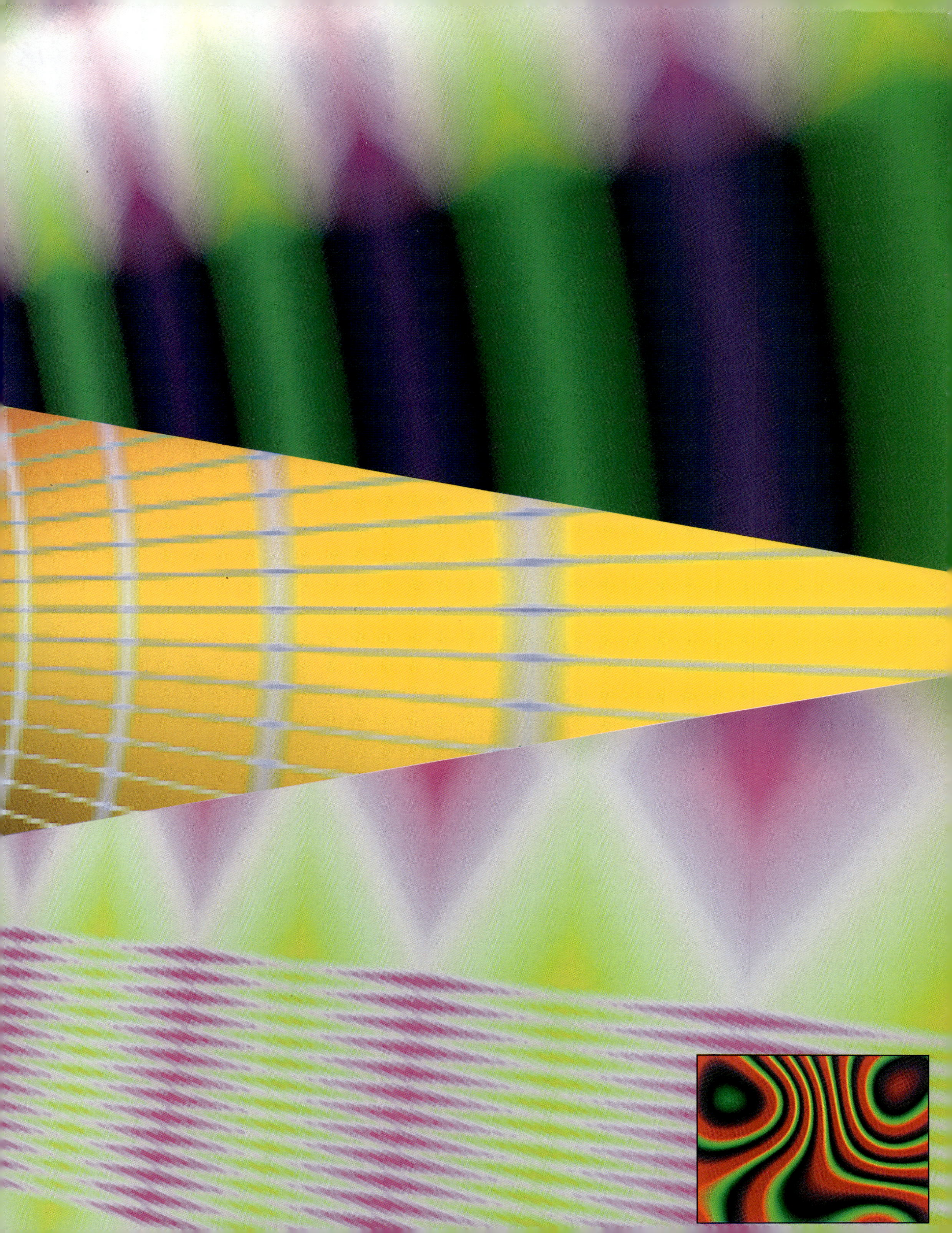

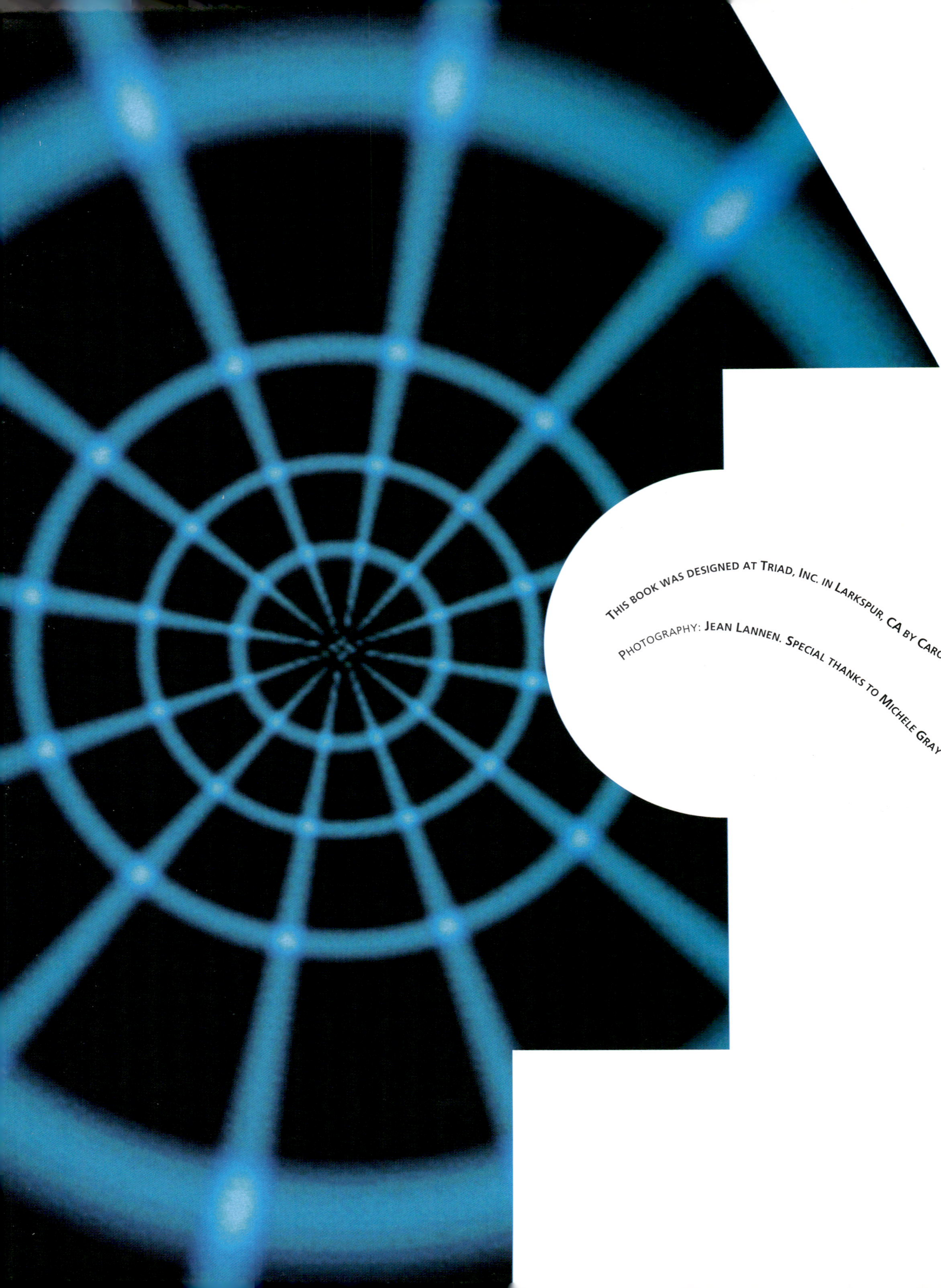

This book was designed at Triad, Inc. in Larkspur, CA by Carol Hoove

Photography: Jean Lannen. Special thanks to Michele Gray for image

IZA VAN GERBIG AND MICHAEL DAMBROWSKI.

ULTIVATION AND NURTURING THIS PROJECT TO FRUITION.

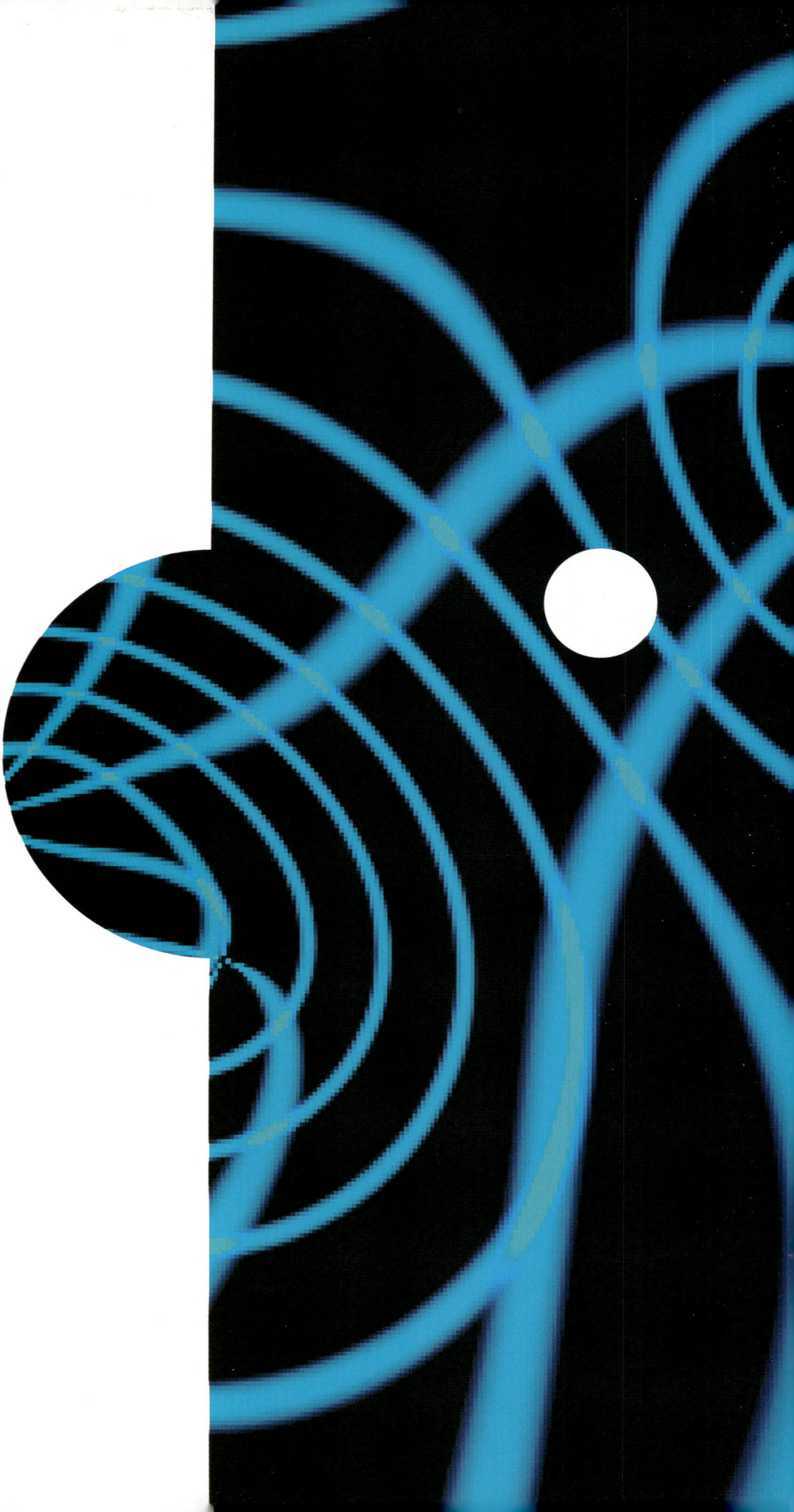

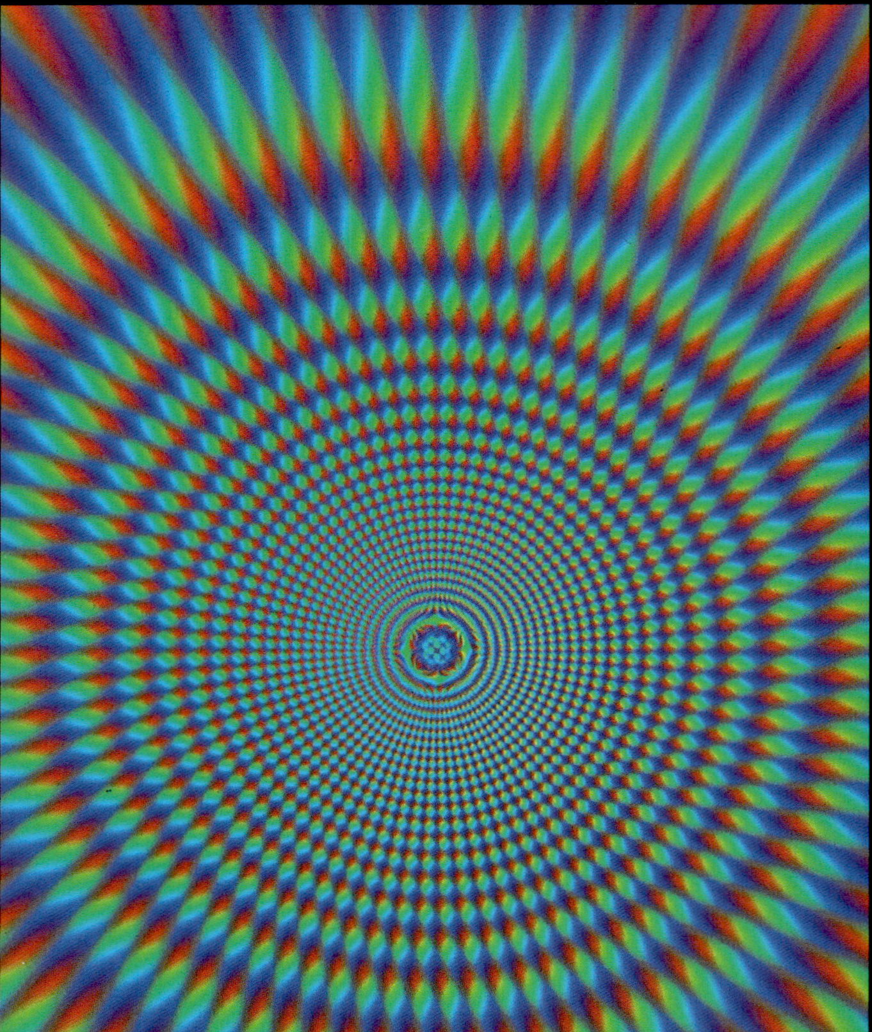